How to Use Marketing Techniques to Get a Great Job

How to Use Marketing Techniques to Get a Great Job

Your Key to a Great Career

Edward Barr

BEP

BUSINESS EXPERT PRESS

Leader in applied, concise business books

How to Use Marketing Techniques to Get a Great Job:
Your Key to a Great Career

Copyright © Business Expert Press, LLC, 2022.

Cover design by Charlene Kronstedt

Interior design by Exeter Premedia Services Private Ltd., Chennai, India

First published in 2021 by
Business Expert Press, LLC
222 East 46th Street, New York, NY 10017
www.businessexpertpress.com

ISBN-13: 978-1-63742-141-3 (paperback)
ISBN-13: 978-1-63742-142-0 (e-book)

Business Expert Press Business Career Development Collection

Collection ISSN: 2642-2123 (print)
Collection ISSN: 2642-2131 (electronic)

First edition: 2021

10 9 8 7 6 5 4 3 2 1

Description

When we apply for a job, we are essentially trying to sell ourselves. If we understand the process of marketing, we can make that sale a lot easier. This requires a plan that includes a deep understanding of our target audiences, an understanding of our strengths and weaknesses, an understanding of the benefits we can offer, and a knowledge of the 4 Ps, product, place, price and promotion.

Add to this, an ability to differentiate and position ourselves in the crowded marketplace and to use promotional tactics to rise to the top of the applicant pool, we can get the job of our dreams. When we master these skills, we make the chore of getting a great job, the job we want, more a certainty than a hopeful wish.

This book will show you how to network better, how to create an effective email pitch, write a powerful resume and cover letter, and how to persuade recruiters that you offer the most value to satisfy their needs. This book will make you a pro at marketing yourself!

Keywords

marketing; sales; promotion; product; positioning; differentiation; objectivity; attention; action; branding; SWOT; resume; cover letter; email; storytelling; questions; quotes; statistics; blogs; twitter; social media; action; benefit

Contents

Acknowledgments

To my wife, Holly Welty-Barr, who makes the good things in my life possible and who lent me unending support and invaluable advice in writing this book. Also, to Scott Isenberg who believed in the book and Vilma Barr who reviewed it and offered valuable editing advice for improving the text. I thank you.

Introduction

For the past 40 years, I have been a marketing and marketing communications professional and teacher. I have worked as a marketing executive in health care, in video production, in higher education, and in software manufacturing. In that time, I have had many successes and a few failures. I have learned from my mistakes and from the mistakes of others. I have also hired my share of employees.

I have been a Chief Marketing Officer at a Carnegie Mellon University for-profit, iCarnegie, and a VP of Marketing for a group of physicians, Allegheny University Medical Practices (AUMP) with over 280 physicians in over 80 groups. I have also served as a marketing and fund development consultant and taught at colleges and universities in and around Pittsburgh, PA. I have taught "Marketing the Social Enterprise" as a full-time Associate Professor at the H. John Heinz College of Public Policy and Management at Carnegie-Mellon. The Heinz College is one of the top-rated schools of public policy and management in the world and its students among the brightest. I most recently serve as Communication Coach for financial engineering students in the Master of Computational Finance program (MSCF) at CMU. MSCF is consistently ranked in the top five such programs in the world. My students come from China, India, Japan, Italy, and other countries and they are among the brightest in the word. I work with them to help them succeed at networking, interviewing, and communicating on the job in financial institutions in America, Asia, and Europe.

Throughout the years, I have hosted many college students, both in my classes and in my offices, as student interns and full-time employees. I have looked at many eager faces, many resumes, and an equal amount of cover letters. I've interviewed hundreds of people in job interviews and mock interviews. And, I've seen just about every bad mistake that can be made by someone trying to get a job, especially a first job. By the way, I have also been out of work a couple of times and had to scramble to find a new job to pay the mortgage and the car payment, as well as the food and credit cards. Yes, I have been where you are, on the outside looking in, wondering how in God's name to get a job. I've read the job sites just like you, typed cover letters, sent e-mails, and waited for the e-mail to ping or the phone to ring, wondering why the heck it hadn't. I've seen the problem from both sides. I know of what I speak. That's another reason why I am so qualified to talk about this subject.

When I taught marketing, (and I have also taught public relations, corporate communications, presentation skills, negotiation, advertising, and professional writing), I included a session on self promotion. It was the most popular session of the classes and it helped me achieve good student evaluations.

In my teaching, many of my students are intrigued by what I say. Many are dumbfounded, a few are outraged, and a few more think I'm crazy. What I present to my students, and what isn't typical, I hereby present to you in these pages—fundamentals about how to get a job using marketing techniques, the same techniques that are used to sell the beer you drink, the cereal you buy, the cars you drive, the clothes you wear, and even the doctors you visit. These marketing fundamentals and marketing techniques help you identify yourself as a great product, differentiate yourself from your competition, and then sell yourself to a potential employer, based on the benefits you offer them, the needs and wants that you fulfill.

In the next pages, we'll look at how to use tested marketing techniques to get a job, even if you're still in college, how to evaluate the job market, how to examine the job sites, how to write a good e-mail and a good cover letter and resume, and how to interview well.

Ultimately, you'll see that this is all common sense, not some academic voodoo. You'll find that you really do understand marketing from the practical level. It doesn't take a genius to figure it out, just someone who's willing to stand out in the crowd and not listen to the tired, old clichés being force-fed by some people that you should "do what everyone else does and don't make any waves," or "don't look different." This is the very worst advice anyone can give you about getting a job. If Procter & Gamble worked that way, they wouldn't have as many leading products as they do.

As you will see in the following pages, you need to be unique, different from the competition, and offering some benefit to the consumer (the company that you want to hire you). You need to understand and relate to your market! You need to use marketing techniques!

So, hop on for the ride and see what you think!

CHAPTER 1

What Is Marketing?

According to Philip Kotler, the world's guru of marketing, "Marketing is a social and managerial process by which individuals and groups obtain what they need and want through creating and exchanging products of value with others." He also said this, "Marketing is the homework we do before we have a product.[1]" The American Marketing Association defines marketing as "the activity, set of institutions, and processes for creating, communicating, delivering, and exchanging offerings that have value for customers, clients, partners, and society at large.[2]" For years, others defined marketing as the four Ps: product, price, place, and promotion. (Other Ps were later added to that definition, such as "positioning" and "politics.") Regardless of the definition, great marketing is customer-focused. That means great marketers are dedicated to sensing, serving, and satisfying the wants and needs of customers, as Kotler also said. This leads to high customer satisfaction. Great marketers know that if they take care of their customers, market share and profits will follow. This means creating customer value and satisfaction.

Marketing Is Objectivity

A legendary ad man, David Ogilvy, attributed this concept—"Marketing Is Objectivity"—to one of his colleagues. No truer words were ever spoken. No complicated process was ever narrowed to such a succinct phrase. To succeed in marketing, you must view the buy-sell exchange from the buyer's (or in this case, the employer's) point of view, not your subjective point of view. Because we are all motivated by self-interest, we find it nearly impossible to be objective, to think "outside-in" instead of

---

[1] https://coursehero.com/file/45170930/INTRO-TO-MARKETINGdoc/
[2] https://ama.org/the-definition-of-marketing-what-is-marketing/

"inside-out." But, to succeed, we must leave our egos behind and think like the other.

Whoever is buying something from you is interested in what the product can do for them, not what is intrinsically right or different or cool about the product. The buyer wants to know, "What will this do for me?" Or, they'll want an answer to that magical acronym, WIFM (What's in it for me?). It's a fine distinction, learning to switch your perspective away from yourself and to the employer, but it's a distinction you must reconcile. The buyer is not really interested in you, as such. She's interested in what the product (detergent, perfume, shampoo, a sports car, you) can do for her. In other words, in the case of a job candidate, she's interested in how you, the candidate, can solve her problem, her immediate problem. In the case of a job, she wants to know where to find a warm body to do the work she's likely been doing since the last person left to go somewhere else. If you're objective, you'll understand her plight. You'll be more interested in her (objective) than in yourself (subjectivity).

Keep this concept in mind; it's a cornerstone of getting a job and succeeding in any marketing venture. As David Ogilvy was told, "Marketing Is Objectivity.[3]" It's not what you want that's important, it's who I am, the person with the job to offer, and what I need that's important.

Do You Know Your Customer

To know the customer is the most important marketing rule but it has become almost a cliché and devoid of meaning. What does it mean to know your customer? It means actually empathizing with your customer, you know, walking a mile in her moccasins, knowing what the heck she's going through, what she needs.

For instance, the best way to get a date with the person with whom you're most interested is to understand what motivates that person, what she or he values. You know, like "Men are from Mars—Women are from Venus." If you're a man and you're looking for a relationship with that special person, you better be ready to listen and relate. If you're a woman and you want to find that special person, you better understand something about the topics

---

[3] https://marketingbyred.com/marketing/ogilvy-on-advertising-by-david-ogilvy/

that interest that person. "Know thyself" is good advice; it guides you in choosing a person that suits your interests, but it won't get you a relationship with the person who interests you. And, it won't get you customers as a marketing person or a job as a potential employee. For that, you must "Know Them," know the customer, the person, and the company that will hire you.

Knowing the customer (Hiring Person) means knowing what she needs and using that knowledge to attract her attention. There are prospective employers out there who are interested in punk hair and pink cover letters and resumes. If you happen to look and act that way, you may be a good fit for an Art Director at an Ad Agency or PR firm. If you're a graphic designer who can make great designs, then, by all means, go for pink and punk, if that's your color and your style. Otherwise, especially if you're looking for work at the local bank, stay away from the less conservative in dress and manner.

Knowing your customer (let's say it's a bank) means knowing that it doesn't hire people with unusual demeanor. It means knowing it will automatically dismiss any resume that is awkward piece of pink paper sticking out of an otherwise trim and manageable pile of papers. Knowing your customer means knowing that the person who will review your credentials is overwhelmed with stuff to do, stuff that's going to have to wait while she reads letters and resumes, and then chooses 10 or 12 people to interview, develops an interview format, schedules interviews, suffers through them, and consults with her colleagues. She will then make her hiring decision. Knowing your customer means knowing she'll rely on her new hire (you) to immediately become a member of the team, be self-motivated, perform the essential tasks, not embarrass her in front of the executives, and show the execs that she's a manager who knows how to choose the candidate who can contribute to the success of the organization.

Knowing your customer is critical. This rule is so obvious that it almost seems silly to repeat; yet, every day not just job hunters but major corporate vice presidents (and vice presidents of marketing) ignore it, all in the name of subjectivity, a focus on their own ideas, what they think is important. Subjectivity is good; it helps us stay alive, but it doesn't help us sell much. Marketing is objectivity. Just because we have invented what we believe is a great product (and it might even *be* a great product) doesn't mean anyone will buy it. If you ever want to test subjectivity, ask a bunch of women who have had children if their babies were ugly. We all know there are ugly babies, but they are someone else's babies. No woman, or man for that matter, will ever say their baby is ugly. They are very subjective about the issue.

Knowing your customer (Prospective Employer) means knowing just what job she needs someone to handle and making her confident, through your cover letter, resume, and interview, that you're the one to handle it. This means taking an objective approach, looking at the job from the other's point of view.

Marketers can never know enough about their customers. You, too, need to know as much as possible about your customer so that you can determine what they want, what they value, and then position yourself as the person who can deliver that value. Who is your customer when you are looking for a job? Obviously, the employer. You can easily learn as much as you want about any employer, the company, and the people in it. Technology has made that easy. We're talking about more information than the job as described in a job announcement. You can use public documents on the Internet to learn much about the companies you have targeted, their values, their customers, their workforce, and their financial status. If you are trying to learn about the people who might interview you, you can use social media to learn as much as you can about the media they use, how often they use that media, what interests them, and more. Facebook and LinkedIn will likely give you all you need. You can also network to find people within the organization who can give you tips and advice. It only requires you to act.

Understand this, though. Your potential employer can also learn a lot more about you. The employer has the same easy access to information and can learn about your habits, your values, and your relationships, just as you can learn about theirs.

Most people are spending as much as 10 hours each day on a screen (Deloitte), the one on their desk or the one in their pocket. Adults are checking their phones as many as 46 times each day; that's nearly three times a waking hour[4] (eight billion times per day). People and companies are doing a lot of posting. You will find much about them.

---

[4] https://time.com/4147614/smartphone-usage-us-2015/

Your potential employer will have a brand image. The Internet and social media are going to reveal that image. What colors do they use? What typefaces? What photos? What does their content focus on? What key words and subject matter are they showing on their Facebook, Instagram, Twitter, and LinkedIn pages? Speaking of social media, is your Facebook page filled with pictures of you skiing? Bungee jumping? Traveling? Partying? Volunteering in homeless shelters? What kind of language do you use? Do you post to Instagram? If so, what kinds of photos are you putting there? Are you posting videos to TikTok? Do you have a WeChat account?

You are a matter of public record, just as they are. Most employers are using social media to vette you. If you've embarrassed yourself with inappropriate remarks regarding race, gender, religion, or politics, you may want to go back into your posts and delete some of them.

Can You Help Your Customer Avoid Pain?

Understand this about your audiences, the employers, everyone: We are all driven by these goals, seeking pleasure, and avoiding pain. What does that mean in this context? When someone interviews you, she wants the experience to be a good one, perhaps even enjoyable. She wants to feel as if she is not wasting her time. She wants to predict that you will be a great employee because of your warmth and competence. She wants you to know about her and her company; that is pleasurable. She doesn't want you to stumble around and embarrass yourself because then she will feel embarrassed. That is painful.

Do You Know the Picture of the Successful Employee?

Get a clear notion of what is required to succeed at the company you are targeting. Talk to people who work there. Get informational interviews with managers there and ask them about the qualities and behaviors of their best employees. You cannot do enough research and planning when you are trying to secure a job. Any successful marketer must know as much as possible about her potential customer. For that reason, marketing firms conduct research and conduct focus groups. However, neuroscience has proven that we don't always know why we behave the way we do. We have "behavioral biases" and we are both affected by and affect others with framing, priming, loss aversion, risk aversion, availability heuristics, and many other significant biases.

Are You Like Them?

In his fascinating book, *Influence*, author Robert Cialdini listed six forms of persuasion: social proof, reciprocity, commitment, scarcity, authority, and liking.[5] He has since added another form of persuasion, "Unity."

We can be persuaded by what others are doing (social proof), by the giving and receiving of gifts or aid (reciprocity), by commitments that we have made and act consistently to (commitment), by unavailability of items or services (scarcity), by titles and trappings (authority), and by similarities (liking). In regard to this last one, Cialdini said that we can be influenced by people who are like us. We may have the same first name, we may have the same background, we may come from the same hometown, we may dress alike, or we may be alike in many other ways. Cialdini and his colleagues demonstrated through their research the power of liking.

So, what does this mean to you who are trying to get a job? It means that you need to quickly understand the way people dress at the company you are applying to. It means that you need to understand the way they talk. It means you need to quickly find out the many other ways you can match them, be like them. And, as you discover this information, you must also decide if the company fits the image of who you are.

Do You Understand Their Brains?

These days all marketers need to understand the fundamentals of how the brain functions. At its most basic level, the so-called lizard brain regulates your breathing, body temperature, sleeping, heart rate, digestion, and other normal body functions. Your brain also has a small walnut-shaped cluster of neurons called the amygdala. It regulates your fight or flight

---

[5] https://socialmediaexaminer.com/6-powerful-social-media-persuasion-techniques/

reaction. Another area, the so-called limbic brain, contains neurons related to emotions of all kinds. The neo-cortex sits on top of the brain and consists of neurons that help you with higher functions, such as planning. This is collectively called the "triune brain" and is meant as a metaphor just as Daniel Kahneman's book, *Thinking, Fast and Slow* discusses "System 1" and "System 2," both metaphors (or homunculi, as he calls them).

In any event, much has begun to be written about the brain, and the triune brain idea has been debunked by many neuroscientists. The brain has been accurately described as a "network" much like the Internet. In any event, we are known by most neuroscientists to live our lives mostly nonconsciously suggesting that most of what we do occurs at a nonconscious level. We drive from here to there and don't remember exactly how we got there. We develop neural pathways that help us do many things automatically, without "thinking." This, in turn, leads us to make mistakes. We call some of these mistakes "behavioral biases." One such bias is called "confirmation bias."

Do You Know About Biases?

When we suffer conformation bias, we tend to interpret new evidence as confirmation of our existing beliefs or theories. What does that mean to you? It suggests that your customer (the employer) will form an impression of you very quickly (existing belief) and then spend the rest of the time in your presence trying to confirm that existing impression. In other words, if they meet you and dislike you, they may look for reasons to prove and justify that feeling. It certainly makes your first impression an important one. We'll talk more about that when we discuss a critical piece of marketing, the product. For marketers who deal with pricing and placement, these biases are critical to understand.

Do You Know About Framing and Priming?

We will take a brief look at some other behaviors. For instance, for our purposes, we should know a little bit about framing and priming as they might help us land the job we seek.

Framing relates to the manner in which you present information. For instance, if you say that 95 percent of the people who try a product love it while 5 percent hate it, that's a lot different from saying that 5 percent of the people who try a product hate it although 95 percent like it. It's obviously a matter of emphasis but it affects the way people perceive a product. Likewise, you need to think about how you present yourself, especially the language that you use to present yourself. What will you emphasize? If audiences remember the first things they are told, what do you want to say first? How will you frame yourself? Will you be the Carnegie Mellon graduate who spent two years in the Peace Corps, or the Peace Corps volunteer who graduated from Carnegie Mellon University? The emphasis makes a difference.

Priming relates to the things you say before, or during, your meeting with a prospective employer. Words have power. If you use words such as excellence, top notch, stellar, spectacular, and so on, you will be priming your audience to make similar associations with you. Research has shown that test subjects exposed to words such as old, elderly, Florida and so forth walked away from a test more slowly, simply because their minds were connecting to words for the elderly. When your brain hears a word, it associates it with other related words in a process called "spreading activation." You want your words to spread to areas of the brain related to excellence and other positive characteristics.

Key Concepts

Marketing is objectivity.

Successful marketing senses, serves, and satisfies the wants and needs of customers.

You can never know enough about your customers.

Your potential employer is your customer.

Employers want to avoid pain by hiring well.

Our brains sometimes respond with biases.

**What Do You Know About Your Customer
(Potential Employer)**

What pains them?_____

What is their culture?_____

What motivates them?_____

What characteristics do they seek in an employee?_____

How can you provide them with benefits?_____

CHAPTER 2

The "4 P's"

Product, Price, Place, and Promotion

Marketing has been greatly misunderstood for years. When I ask my classes to define marketing, they invariably define it as "sales," or "promotion," or "PR." Marketing is these things, but it is also much, much more.

Essentially, marketing is an exchange. I, the employer, give up money, benefits, and security to you, the employee, in exchange for services, the quality work that you perform everyday on my behalf. That's an exchange.

But, marketing uses many techniques to manage this exchange. Many people know marketing as the "4 P's." These "P's" stand for (1) Product, (2) Price, (3) Place, and (4) Promotion. (The "4 P's" have been expanded in some circles to the "5 P's" and even the "6 P's," but we won't worry ourselves here about such academic matters, except to say that the other P's are positioning and politics.)

Let's face it, when you try to get a job, you're trying to market yourself, a product, to another person. Think about that. You're offering a great *product*, yourself (you must believe you're a great product) at a reasonable *price*, negotiable (that is, you're willing to discuss salary), easily *distributed* (that is, most of you will travel to any *place* and you're available upon request, just name the time and place), and you have certain promote-able characteristics (you're distinctive from the rest, the competition.) If you agree you're a "product," then you will agree that you can use marketing tools and marketing thinking to get that great job you deserve.

If at this moment you scream, "But I didn't study marketing at college!" Forget it. You don't need to be experienced, schooled, or degreed in marketing. Heck, I don't even have a degree in marketing, but I've been a marketing executive and have taught marketing in one of the most prestigious universities in the world. Better that you aren't a marketing expert, in most cases. Nothing is as common as marketing people who don't market themselves and don't know how to get a job. They're like the shoemaker whose kids have holes in their shoes.

As I said before, marketing is simple common sense, really. If you want to be a good marketer, you only need to pay attention to some very basic notions of human nature and pay attention to what works best in making you buy a product like Coke, Pepsi, Nike, Polo, Tide, Crest, and so on. Proctor and Gamble, Disney, the others I just mentioned are the world's best marketers. You only need to watch what they do and then adapt to those techniques to market yourself.

I can tell you this: most counselors won't teach you about marketing yourself. They don't understand, and, therefore, they disregard these techniques. They'll be the first ones to warn you not to do the things I recommend in this book. So, check out the following pages and decide for yourself. After all, it's your job we're talking about.

Key Concepts

Marketing has traditionally been known as the "4 P's."

Marketing is more than sales and advertising; it is an exchange.

To market successfully, one must create a great product that serves a need.

Prices effect how people buy.

Some jobs require movement and relocation; this refers to place in the 4 P's.

Promotion is the most visible "P" in the marketer's portfolio.

CHAPTER 3

A Great Product— the First "P"

What Do You Bring to The Table?

When marketers begin to plan, they develop a "Marketing Mix." This includes all of the things we will be talking about, in depth, in the following pages. They will create a promotional strategy of sales, advertisements, giveaways, and other such tactics. They will decide on prices. They will consider the means of distributing their product. But, their first consideration must be the product.

OK, the first of the Ps is "Product." And, you have accepted that you are the product. You have also accepted that you must be objective about that product and understand it from the eyes of the customer, the hiring agent. Well, let me tell you a story about a failure to be objective and understand the buyer.

I was once involved with what I thought was a great product, a 100 percent rubber booty for horses, kind of a "spare tire" for use if the horse threw a shoe. My partners and I thought it was a great concept and guaranteed to be the next hula hoop. Why did we feel that way? Well, there was no such product on the market. It was incredibly unique. We owned the rights to distribute the shoe in the 25 states east of the Mississippi. The shoe wasn't expensive or difficult to warehouse and we already had contacts with major distributors of equestrian equipment and large tack houses. Then, we multiplied the number of horses by four and found that number to be huge! We saw ourselves (the three of us) as wealthy business people.

We could find no problems with our product. We were in love with it (we were extremely subjective). Rubber booties seemed a more humane way to shoe a horse than with nails. We felt we had great selling points.

To wit: Very few products are made of 100 percent pure rubber. Even your car tires are synthetic. A farrier/blacksmith invented our product. Veterinarians used our rubber horseshoe in their treatment of horses; the vets loved it. If they had to sedate a horse, our booty was ideal for the moment the horse regained consciousness and struggled to its feet. It was perfect for horses on concrete, on parade, or on show in a mall.

We were psyched. We saw dollars signs everywhere. We tested the product with the Amish and acquired their endorsement. We printed glossy brochures with a sexy, young woman on a horse. We counted our profits before we sold any product, we made plans to buy summer homes in Belize and new Teslas. In other words, we were greatly subjective.

Unfortunately, after months of trying to hustle the shoes, we found that no one wanted to buy them. We were dumbfounded. What had we done wrong? Well, for one thing we didn't invest in any research to find the values, attitudes, behaviors, and beliefs of our potential customers. We learned the hard way that people who own horses weren't ready to give up on thousands of years of traditional shoeing. We would have known that if we had not been so much in love with our own creation, so subjective. We wasted a lot of time and money and finally gave up the business.

So, what does this mean to you, the unemployed or underemployed person, not the horseshoe hustler, the person who wants a job, or wants a better job. More than anything, it means you must be ready to give the customer (the potential employer) something he or she wants/needs. The fact that you are unemployed means nothing. You must make yourself into a product for which the customer can find some benefit. It means that you must be objective, not subjective.

You must relate everything about the marketing of yourself to this truth. You must, ironically, be objective about yourself, not subjective, in the most overtly subjective tools—the resume and the cover letter (more on this later). And, you must think objectivity in the interview. In my work with students and others who come to me for mock interviews and advice on landing a job, I find this to be akin to a paradigm shift!

But, what "product" do employers want? I can't speak for everyone, but I wanted these product attributes or benefits:

Product Attributes Aka Benefits

Self-Motivation

I always looked for people who were eager, enthusiastic, ambitious, and ready to hit the ground running. I wanted to have to chase them to slow them down. I wanted them to go forward and make some mistakes. I didn't want to have to jumpstart them every morning. I wanted them to want *my* job.

Why did I look for these kinds of people? I knew that when they succeeded, I succeeded. I wanted to be known as the person who chose the best talent. I was not afraid of their taking my job. I was more concerned about another company hearing about them and pirating them. But, I also felt very proud when they were hired away in positions higher than the ones they had in my organization. I felt as if I had mentored them. It was a good feeling. As a result, I can't imagine an employer not wanting these kinds of people. As a matter of fact, I'd always suggest that anyone who has this kind of self-motivation steer clear of employers and managers who feel threatened by them.

Strong Ethics

Every job gives people the opportunity to be unethical. Some sales people offer gifts, petty cash drawers remain open, offices being swept at night display critical information. It's not easy to discern whether or not a person has strong ethics but behavioral interview questions help. When you are asked a behavioral question regarding your ethics, you need to be prepared to demonstrate, in some way, probably through storytelling, that you are an ethical person. It also helps to have recommendations in hand or on LinkedIn from people who can attest to your honesty.

Maturity

Here, again, you can prove your maturity in several ways. Your cover letter and resume reflect maturity, or lack thereof. If you write a sloppy cover letter and a disorganized resume, it hurts your brand (much more on this later). If you dress poorly or have hygiene issues, you will not be seen as mature.

Mostly, though, your past experiences will give clues to your maturity. What projects have you worked on? How did you approach them? Again, behavioral questions can reveal your level of maturity. For instance, you will likely be asked, "Tell me about a time when you disagreed with your boss?" or, "Tell me about a time when you had a conflict with a co-worker." You have a chance here to be a masterful storyteller. You can use the STAR process: Situation, Task, Action, Result. In the interview, you will make a first impression. You want that to be powerful. You will look more mature by dressing conservatively, grooming yourself well, standing erect with your shoulders back and your chin level, making good eye contact, giving a firm handshake, and speaking in a mid-range tone, not too high pitched.

Teamwork

More than ever, workplaces have flattened organizational charts and work is done by self-directed teams. That means teams must function smoothly together. They must trust each other, communicate fluidly, and accept responsibility for agreed-upon outcomes. In promoting yourself (much more on this to come), you need to position yourself as a team player, a mature, ethical, and self-motivated team player.

Experience

Of course, employers want the benefit of a candidate with experience. They want to know that you've been in the fire and not just survived but thrived. You will have plenty of opportunities to show that. Keep in mind they will want to hear the STAR: situation, task, action, and result. They will especially want to know the result. They will want it to be quantifiable, measureable, in dollars and cents, in time, and perhaps in customer satisfaction. Your promotional materials (much more on this to come) and the interview will allow you to reveal this.

Balance

Employers want balanced workers. You may think they want you to work 16 hours each day, and they may not complain if you do, but they will expect you to maintain balance. If you have a miserable home life, your work will suffer. If you have poor health, your work will suffer. You need some yin with your yang (old Chinese balance principles). I knew one person, a managing director at an international bank, Devin, who goes right to the bottom of resumes to see what activities candidates enjoy. He wants to know what makes them individuals since all of the resumes he received essentially say the same thing: math, statistics, economics, coding—all A's and A+s. He likes to question the people who say they like bungee jumping or snorkeling, or competitive shooting. It also gives him a lot more information about personalities: "You like bungee jumping? You must also like risk. Talk to me about this."

Empathy

These days emotional intelligence is highly valued by executives and managers. And, rightly so. If you have no empathy, for instance, you will be unable to fully understand your customers and your colleagues. Having feeling for a co-worker, customer or relative living through a serious illness, or recovering from the death of a loved one, will make a difference. I had an associate who was hit by a car while walking to work. She suffered a head injury that was misdiagnosed initially and she received no support from her supervisors who called her continuously at home asking when she would return to work. When she recovered, she immediately began to seek another job.

Making the Boss Look Good

When I hired people, I wanted them to make me look good, not because of egotistical reasons, but as confirmation that I had hired well. I, in turn, tried to make my boss look good. And, she tried to make her boss look good, and so on, ad infinitum. Being able to do that meant so many things: an understanding and acceptance of the organization's mission and values, a set of goals that fit the organization's strategic plan, accomplishment of those goals, an ability to achieve stretch goals, passion, energy, enthusiasm, commitment, courage, and other such traits. When I interviewed candidates, I also asked other team members to interview the candidates; we came together and discussed our observations. I made the final decision. Sometimes I was right and sometimes I wasn't. No interview can truly reveal the person who has applied. But, as a candidate you must reveal that you possess these attributes (benefits). When you do, you are more likely to get the job. You will be seen as the most desirable "product."

You might add other strong benefits such as those already mentioned and that's OK. The important thing is for you to stress these attributes; stress them in your cover letter, resume, and interview comments, as well as the letters of reference you receive from other people.

What Price Will You Charge—Your Salary— the Second "P"

Everybody has a price, they say. And, you will surely be asked yours (or told the limits). Your price, of course, is your salary expectation. Michael Porter, Harvard's guru of strategy, said that businesses have only three strategies: cost leadership, niche, and differentiation.[1] Here we talk about cost leadership and how you, as a product and business, sell yourself.

If I understand Porter correctly, by cost leadership he meant both low cost and high cost. So, when we think of low cost, whom do we think of? Walmart, of course. When we think of high cost, we may think of Gucci, Rolls Royce, Ralph Lauren, Prada, maybe even Nordstrom. You, as a product, have your choice to choose either, low or high, just like these other products.

You could make it understood that, because you are so excited and want to work for them worse than anything, you will accept the minimum pay if you are offered the job. You might become the low cost leader among the candidates. Why would you do this? To get experience either at the beginning of your career or to make a career change. Of course, every job probably has a salary range that employers try to stay within. In fact, you may be told, going in, that the job begins at a certain salary. But, you always have other nonsalary financial choices.

---

[1] https://ifm.eng.cam.ac.uk/research/dstools/porters-generic-competitive-strategies/

Candidates can always negotiate, even before they have been offered a position. It's an interesting tactic, to begin by saying, "Hire me and you will get the bargain of a lifetime, exceptional talent at low cost." It's a strategy. And, you could also say, "I have the best talent among your candidates and expect to be brought into the job above the mid-point." You need to decide what strategy suits you. Even if you say nothing, that's a strategy (not a very good one).

Keep in mind when, and if, you negotiate, that you need not get stuck on salary issues. You can always negotiate around nonsalary matters: student loans, moving expenses, six month bonuses, and so on.

This is all part of the price component of marketing. All businesses need to adopt a pricing strategy and know their audience extremely well. Some businesses pay top salaries to attract and hire only the very best candidates. Other businesses cannot afford to adopt this strategy. You could make a strategic error by using the wrong tactic. But, why would you ever leave this critical piece to chance. Salaries are table stakes, the cost of getting into the game. Once you're in the game (have the job), salary becomes less important. Other factors take over, especially "Do I like my boss?" Most people leave a job because they don't like their manager. Many other nonsalary issues also come into play.

Give a thought to your salary requirements and, above all, don't short-change yourself. Get out of your own way. Know that most businesses today depend on skilled people; machines haven't taken over yet. If you take all of the people away from Deloitte, McKinsey, Carnegie Mellon, Microsoft, and many other big brands, you will be left with empty buildings. People make this world go around. Believe in yourself and your talents. Price yourself accordingly. If you don't, why should anyone else?

Where Will You Deliver the Product/Service— Place—the Third "P"

Many marketers must think of the ways available to distribute (place) their products. Obviously there is much to consider, logistics, supply chains, transportation costs, and so on. Ultimately, your toilet paper makes its way from the mill to the grocery store. It passes through (not a pun) many stages before it gets into your hands (also not a pun). Other products make their way through Etsy, Amazon, eBay, and other online channels. Indeed, "channel" is a word marketing people are quite familiar with. They consider it a vital part of their marketing mix.

When I was a Chief Marketing Officer at iCarnegie, a Carnegie Mellon University (CMU) for-profit selling CMU learning around the world, we had a small staff in Pittsburgh and we depended on "channel partners" in other countries to bring our message and our products to the right audiences.

For the purpose of marketing yourself to a potential employer, you must think of place as your decision regarding the place(s) where you will work. You need to make that decision early on. It will affect the companies you choose to target and the line of work you adopt.

If you wish to become a consultant, you will likely be placed anywhere and for various periods of time. Knowing that the job involves travel or relocation, you will then address your willingness to travel or locate in your cover letter, or certainly in your interviews.

Obviously, if you care not to travel or relocate, you will avoid jobs that require this. So, the "P" called "place" need not trouble you or cause you a lot of energy when creating your marketing strategy. You will either move/travel or not. (Although it occurs to me that you could negotiate somewhere in between.) Also, you may be willing to travel in the early years of life when you are not involved in a relationship and don't have a family. Perhaps later you will need the stability of not traveling. You may also be willing to live in certain areas early in your career, in a big city, for instance, but not later when you have other commitments, for instance, a family. Different locations obviously have different costs, so refer to your short- and long-term goals when making this decision.

We have discussed three of the "Ps:" Product, Price, and Place. The one that will be most familiar to us and in many ways allow us the greatest creativity and flexibility is "Promotion." Let's move on to that. There's a lot to talk about!

How Will You Promote the Product/Service? Promotion—the Fourth "P"

When most people think of marketing, they think of promotion and sales. Of course, why not? They are the most visible parts of the marketing mix.

Although promotion is nearly impossible to do without, Philip Kotler has said, *"Today's smart marketers don't sell products; they sell benefit packages."* He also said, "The best advertising is done by satisfied customers.[2]" Peter Drucker, a world famous business consultant, said, "The aim of marketing is to make selling superfluous.[3]"

Let's look at those thoughts a minute before we dig into promotions.

We have begun this discussion with the first "P," Product. I also referred to products as benefits. Here's the cold hard truth: If you don't have a good product that delivers the benefits the customer needs, you will not sell anything successfully. As a product, that is, potential employee, if you make claims to benefits that you can't deliver after someone has purchased (hired) you, they will not buy from you again and they will influence others not to buy from you. They will find ways to dismiss you and denigrate your reputation with their colleagues.

Let's take this back to your trying to get a job. You will need to promote yourself, but you must do it in a way that stresses the benefits that you can actually deliver. Remember, marketing begins with an understanding of the customer (the audience) and their wants and needs. As outlined earlier, most employers want the same things: self-motivation, high ethical standards, teamwork, and so on.

OK, so we agree—you are a product. You have been designed and manufactured (by your parents, your teachers, and yourself) to deliver results, to fill some need in the marketplace, some demand. If you haven't, you may need to start over again. It isn't unusual for people to start over again, to remake themselves in a way that will prepare them for a demand they know to exit, such as software engineer or machine learning specialist. They can then, in effect, make a better product of themselves. I see many students who believe that if they make themselves into computer literate individuals they will become products of great potential value and demand. And, I have taught many adults who are returning to school to acquire the skills they know to be in great demand. In other words, they are improving their product, themselves. They could splash "New" and

---

[2] https://inspiringquotes.us/author/3081-philip-kotler

[3] https://marketinginsidergroup.com/strategy/marketing-is-business-the-wisdom-of-peter-drucker/

"Improved" on their resumes and other promotions, if it weren't unacceptable to their potential customers—and we'll get to that.

Let's say you have identified a need in the marketplace and you have developed a product to satisfy that need, yourself. How, then, do you create the marketing exchange you wish to create—how do you get the potential employer to buy you? Well, pricing will have something to do with it, as will distribution, as we just said; you will have to agree on salary needs and your eventual place of assignment. However, you will never get to those matters until you have caught the attention of your customer (potential employer). Later we will discuss the promotional techniques in depth, including AIDA (Attention, Interest, Desire, Action). But, before we get too far into promoting yourself, let's talk about planning.

Key Concepts

A marketing mix begins with a product or service (you).

Buyers (employers) are looking for benefits.

Employers want people who are self-motivated, ethical, mature, experienced, and team-oriented, among other things.

At some point, price (your salary), place (the location of your office), and promotion (your reputation) will be relevant.

Answer These Questions

What can you offer in benefits that your employer needs?_____

What are your salary expectations?_____

In what locations will you agree to work (and not work)?_____

What is your reputation? (How have you promoted yourself to this point)?_____

CHAPTER 4

You Need a Plan

To succeed in this world, whether it's in a social organization, job search, relationship, or any important endeavor, you need a plan. You really do. You need to think about yourself, about what you want out of life, and about your values and beliefs. You need to examine the environment, look at your strengths and weaknesses, set some objectives, develop some strategies, in short, create a plan.

To create a useful plan, you've got to spend some time thinking. Let's face it, the last thing people like to do is think. Thinking burns calories. Your brain uses at least 20 percent of the glucose in your body. Thinking tires people. For this exercise, I'm not telling you to sit down and write a comprehensive strategic plan for your whole life (unless you want to). But, do some soul searching about what work you want to do for the rest of your life. Do a psychological profile on yourself. Are you an achiever (you must be if you're finishing college), an environmentally conscious person (do you refuse to use Styrofoam), or a slacker? Do you see yourself wearing a suit and tie? Do you see yourself working in an office or does that make you want to run in the opposite direction? Or do you see yourself in jeans and a t-shirt? (I once worked for a video production company where the production crews were pretty much defined by the creativity of their t-shirts. Hats seem to have taken over now.) Is money most important to you? Is freedom, the ability to come and go? Would you like to be your own boss? Think about it. Take half a day in serious thought. Be honest with yourself. List your values and beliefs. A few minutes doing this, before you start a job, will save you some hard times down the road.

In fact, write these things on a piece of paper. Nothing makes your thoughts as concrete as setting them to paper. Nothing is as self-fulfilling as a written plan with Action Steps, which require you to perform certain actions by certain dates. Plans, as I said, are self-fulfilling. Write what you want and you're likely to get it.

Do a SWOT Analysis: Strengths, Weaknesses, Opportunities, Threats

Strengths: List here your greatest strengths. Be liberal and kind to yourself. You may be a nice person. People may like you. You may have the best time in the 5K for your age group. You may type 100 words per minute. Maybe you are great with Word. Perhaps your social media understanding is fantastic and you have 5,000 followers on Instagram. List your degree, your certificates, and your interests. Don't shortchange yourself. Focus on the areas where you excelled. Maybe you have a degree in education and excelled in creating lesson plans but didn't enjoy student teaching. You might focus on planning positions.

Weaknesses: When most people create these lists, their weaknesses are greater than their strengths. We all tend to be a little too hard on ourselves. Just be honest and think in terms of weaknesses that will affect your ability to secure a job and then keep it. Perhaps you have a short attention span; you need a job that involves changing tasks. Perhaps you are introverted; maybe you tend to be impatient. Let's say you don't have good skills with Excel. Think about any issue that might keep you from your dream job.

Opportunities: What opportunities exist for you to capture that dream job? Do you have an uncle who works there? A neighbor? Do any alumni work there? Look everywhere for places you might have an edge to be able to find your perfect workplace. Read the news every day and see how companies are changing. Look for their needs. Look at the macro issues. Is everyone likely to remain in remote jobs? What will that do for you? Does it mean you must change your search in any way?

Threats: These are different from weaknesses. Your ability to work at your dream company may be fading because your skills are going out of style. Is Artificial Intelligence likely to make your skill set less valuable? Are changes brought about by crises, such as a pandemic, likely to necessitate a change in your approach? View the job environment objectively.

Write SMART Objectives

You've assessed yourself objectively. You know your mission in life, your goals, and some strategies. You know the kind of work you want to do and the kind of place where you want to do it. Now, it's time to write some objectives. A plan without objectives cannot be measured.

Your primary goal, of course, is to get the job you want. Your strategies include: writing e-mails, having coffee chats, polishing your cover letter and resume, creating and practicing your elevator pitch, and so on. We will be discussing all of these.

You, also, must write some SMART objectives: What is a SMART objective: one that is Specific, Measurable, Attainable, Relevant, and Time bound.

Here is a SMART objective: "I will write a cover letter and resume by April 1 and have them reviewed by a person whose opinion I respect by April 31."

Here is another SMART objective: "I will send five cover letters and resumes to five key people in the IT industry before the end of May."

Here is another SMART objective: "I will request five LinkedIn connections with five alumni from my school before the end of this month."

I could go on and on writing objectives for getting another job, but I'll spare you. The main point here is to make your actions measurable and accountable. If you say that you will request five LinkedIn connections and don't do it, you only have yourself to blame.

List the Best Strategies

The strategies for getting a job are many. When you have thought through the audience and the benefits that you can provide to them, your differentiation, your branding, your strengths and weaknesses, your positioning, and the means you will use to attract their attention, it's time to employ these strategies: product development (classes), networking, job searching on job sites, e-mail, cover letter, resume, content creation, social media posting, volunteering, and interning.

You're ready

So, you've done a whole afternoon of soul searching down by the beach. You've figured yourself out pretty well. You are an achiever who wants to wear Ann Taylor suits, drive a new SUV, live in a condo near the city, work at a PR firm, and rub elbows with corporate types. You see yourself as the first female CEO from your family. You're willing to start at just above entry level and run on the fast track. Marriage and children can wait a few years. You're headed to the top.

You've written this all down. You've thought about your strengths and weaknesses, you've thought about your uniqueness, you know the competition, you've selected some targets, you've devised some strategies, and you've committed yourself to a number of action steps. You believe in the marketing approach. You're ready to go after the exact job you want.

Key Concepts

Those who fail to plan, plan to fail. Write a plan.

An assessment of your mission, values, and vision is important.

A SWOT analysis will help you clarify your strengths and weaknesses.

SMART objectives will help you define your actions.

Answer These Questions

What is my mission in life?_____

What do I value most?_____

What are my strengths?_____

Where do I need to improve?_____

What strategies can I use to pursue my dreams?_____

Action Plan

Action	Completion Date
Do SWOT analysis	
Write mission, values	
Write SMART objectives	
Create strategies	
Create action plan	

CHAPTER 5

You Must Attract Attention

So, you have a decent understanding of the 4 Ps and you have a plan. Now what?

I recently spoke with a former student who works at a multinational corporation that has offices in Pittsburgh. Brian told me that his company recently received over 400 applications for one communication position. I understand from other students who are looking for jobs and from colleagues who are hiring that this is not unusual. Given this kind of competition, the question is: How does a person beat the odds of 400 to 1 to land that job? By using marketing techniques, of course!

If you are one of four hundred applicants for a position, your most important obligation is attracting attention, you know, sticking out of the crowd, being the one of those 400 resumes and cover letters that is actually read.

Attracting attention is more important than being smart or talented. Heck, most people are average, anyway, maybe a little above average, and the old saying about nothing being as wasted as talent is the truth. Don't worry about your talent or lack thereof. It's better initially to be noticed than to be talented.

Am I talking about attracting attention with a strange hairdo or clothes or an oversized, pink resume, and calligraphy cover letter? No way (unless you want a job as a designer or artist or other creative position). That's not the kind of attention you want to attract. Besides, it violates a cardinal rule of marketing—Know Your Customer.

I'm talking about the kind of attention generated by connecting with the needs of the customer and using strong writing and knowledge of marketing and marketing communications to make that connection. I will expand on this further within this book but for now let's say this: suppose you have bad breath and someone writes to you and says, "Your breath can be fresh all day." Will this attract your attention? Probably, if you have bad breath.

Yes, I know, attracting attention doesn't mean that you (or your product) are credible or will make a sale. It just means that your product (you) has been noticed among all the thousands of other products and their messages (resumes/cover letters) that have been delivered to the employer/customer. Getting attention is (relatively) easy. Getting someone to take action (that is, buy) is a lot harder, as is delivering on the promise.

No one knows this better than Procter & Gamble, Lever Brothers and General Foods, and the many corporations fighting for space and recognition on grocery store shelves. They use distinctive packaging and clever language to attract your attention as you walk the aisles of the grocery store. And, they have already prepared you with hundreds of messages telling you how their products will satisfy your health, beauty, entertainment, or other needs.

You are no different from them when you are trying to make a potential employer notice and appreciate you. How difficult is it to be noticed? Read these statistics from "Wyzowl," a video company:

- According to research, our attention span has markedly decreased in just 15 years. In 2000, it was **12 seconds**…it's shrunk significantly to **8.25 seconds.** In fact, scientists reckon we now have shorter attention spans than goldfish, who are able to focus on a task or object for **9 seconds.**
- Human beings are very, very forgetful…7% of people forget their own birthday from time to time, and studies suggest that each week, 39% of Americans will forget one basic piece of information or lose one every day item.
- Oh, and by the way, we're also easily distracted! An average office worker will check their email inbox 30 times every hour (every two minutes) and will pick up their phones more than 1,500 times per week amounting to 3 hours and 16 minutes a day.
- On the average web page, users will read at most 28% of the words during a visit, with 20% a more likely expectation. The average page visit lasts less than a minute and users often leave web pages in just 10-20 seconds.[1]

---

[1] https://wyzowl.com/human-attention-span/

Yes, the world has an attention-deficit disorder of sorts. When you send your resume, things don't get any better! According to LinkedIn, "Employers only spend about six seconds reading a resume.[2]"

Attracting attention is hard enough, and keeping attention is just as hard. According to the presentation company 2Connect, you can keep the attention of an audience for only seven minutes. They say, "The attention span of a typical audience lasts about 7 minutes before you run the risk of losing them. You might get 10 minutes if the topic is especially of interest, or just 5 minutes if you're lucky enough to be presenting in that sleepy post-lunch period.[3]" Think about the importance of this statement when you go to your next interview. I counsel students to keep their answers short and crisp, using storytelling and the STAR system (situation task, action, result) when appropriate. You don't want to put the audience to sleep!

Will You Read This Article—"an In-Depth Analysis of a Piece of Shit"?

You may or may not read it, depending on a lot of factors: your interest in tropical diseases, your immediate circumstances, and your toleration of four-letter words. But, it will grab your attention. You can't deny that. "Distribution of Schistosoma mansoni and hookworm eggs in human stool[4]" just doesn't have the same (forgive the pun) flavor as the first headline. It isn't going to grab you with its technical jargon. And, Schistosoma mansoni is a very real and very troublesome problem killing lots of people. It deserves to be read and studied by health care workers, government officials, philanthropists, and others who might positively impact the issue.

---

[2] https://linkedin.com/pulse/six-seconds-average-time-spent-reading-resume-andrew-j-friedman/

[3] https://twoconnect.net/7-tips-for-the-7-minute-attention-span/

[4] https://journals.plos.org/plosntds/article?id=10.1371/journal.pntd.0001969

Sometimes We Need To Violate Expectations—Part 1

You weren't ready for the word "shit," were you? It's OK; I feel guilty writing it. But, it gets your attention. And, in a world of 3 million e-mails every second, you need something to get your attention. A website called "Altmetrics" tracks the buzz around scholarly articles and it found that "An in depth analysis … had great buzz and plenty of readers …, one of the highest scores ever in this journal.[5]"

Let's Step Back a Minute

We create messages in our neocortex but the messages must go through the lizard brain of the audience. And, the lizard brain is a cognitive miser; it doesn't want its wattage used for meaningless (in its view) processing. It would rather scan the environment looking for predators, food, foes, or mates. As a result, if you don't play to the lizard brain to attract attention, you will likely be processed out.

How Do You Attract Attention?
Novelty and Disruption

I introduce you to several forms of disruption or novelty: questions, quotes, stories, statistics and novelty, or expectancy violation. They all work! Trust me. They will disrupt and/or present something new to your audience. You can, and should, use them in your e-mails, cover letters, and in networking activity. Later in this book, I give sample cover letters and e-mails that use these techniques. You will see how effective they are.

Ask a Question

Questions by their very nature demand answers. They evoke participation. They are the salesman's greatest tool. Ask any sales person. They create revelations, as in they reveal much about their audience. Questions have been used as successful headlines for years in advertising: "Who loves a baby?"

---

[5] https://altmetric.com/

"Wouldn't you really rather own a Buick?" "Does she or doesn't she? Only her hairdresser knows for sure." "Got milk?" When I say, "Ask a Question," I am advising you to use it in your headline or e-mail subject line. Use it as the first sentence in any communication situation. It will work for you. Why? Because we are built to engage, especially women. Women have four times as many neurons connecting their right and left brain hemispheres and they process through both rational and emotional filters.[6]

Use a Quote

We are suckers for quotes. We treasure the things we don't already know, especially if we are entertained by them or believe they will make us smarter or look better. If you want to look sophisticated, use a simple quote. After all, Da Vinci said, "Simplicity is the ultimate sophistication." The quotes we like best also confirm what we already believe. Use a quote, just as you use a question, as the subject line in an e-mail or the first sentence in an e-mail or cover letter.

Tell a Story

These days everyone is telling stories to show how telling stories is the best business practice since mergers and acquisitions. So, let me tell you a culture story. Once upon a time (ha, stories don't have to begin this way). Anyway, in 2011 I was working for a Carnegie Mellon University (CMU) for-profit company that sold CMU learning around the world, mostly to developing countries and their universities and businesses. As a result, we spent a lot of time in India. Once, the CEO and I visited major business leaders and government officials in Delhi to ask them about the future of STEM (science, technology, engineering, and math) learning in India. We had meetings scheduled all day for several days with the highest-ranking government officials and business leaders. In each meeting something strange was happening, the leadership of India was only addressing me. I was the Chief Marketing Officer, not the boss, but

---

[6] https://sfgate.com/science/article/A-K-Pradeep-mines-the-brain-for-marketers-3166267.php

they kept deferring to me. This was a little irksome to the CEO. Finally, I understood the reason: the CEO was younger than me by 20 years. In India, the culture defers to age to a large extent. The leaders we were meeting assumed that I was older and therefore more important. So, did you like my story? Did I attract and hold your attention? A story doesn't have to be fiction. It needs to be instructive and memorable. And, obviously, you need to understand the culture of your customer.

Many excellent books have been written on storytelling and on storytelling for business. You can begin any written piece, e-mail, cover letter, and so on with a brief story. And, remember to tell stories in your interviews. Stories are remembered.

Use Statistics

Look, 96 percent of all written materials that use statistics are read. Sure, I just used a statistic on you, an invented one. But, it had an effect on you, didn't it? How about this one: 7,000 students drop out of school in America—every day.[7] That one is true, and troublesome, and frightening. It will surely grab your attention if you are an audience member with any interest in our school systems. We will also consider it later when we talk about the importance of using simplicity, plain language, and repetition.

Violate Expectations—Part 2

Patagonia advertised on Black Friday, the busiest shopping day of the year in the United States, NOT to buy their products. They violated all expectations of an advertiser. Yes, you can violate but you must stay believable. Quiznos violated expectations by featuring rats in their advertising as their spokes-rats[8] (they called them "spongmonkies"). That will grab your attention but not in a way that you want your attention to be grabbed. Rats??!! What was Quiznos thinking??? And, how about Protein World? They pictured the body of a very lithe and beautiful young woman and

---

[7] https://dosomething.org/us/facts/11-facts-about-high-school-dropout-rates#fn1

[8] https://en.wikipedia.org/wiki/Quiznos

then asked the world, "Are you beach body ready," suggesting, of course, that only a lithe body is beach-ready.[9] They irritated a lot of women with that disruption. As does the Toilet to Tap movement. Hey, I get it that we need to recycle water, especially in the most arid places, but regardless of how true and hip and cool it is, the Toilet to Tap name just doesn't wash (if you know what I mean).

Beware of the Amygdala Hijack!

You want to grab the attention of your audience by understanding that their lizard brain filters, but you must remember that the amygdala manages fear and its cousin, flight. If you scare the amygdala too much (try rats), it will want to fight or flee. You don't want that to happen. You want positive attention. So, don't tell a story that suggests that you aren't a great person. Don't frighten the recruiter in any way.

Why Do We Love Novelty and Change?

Novelty is a function of "prediction error." But, our brains approach novelty with caution. We have an equally strong need for constancy and commitment. Familiarity is a heuristic (a shortcut). It's the "exposure effect," the more we see something, the more we like it. So, as the man says, "Make the New Familiar and the Familiar New.[10]" The quote is attributed to a Rory Sutherland TED Talk, and it fits with the brain's way of dealing with novelty and surprise.[11] We are well advised to heed that advice.

Creating Interest and Desire

OK, so we're dipping our toes in the subject of promotion, that which most people associate with marketing, and, indeed, a very important part

---

[9] https://theguardian.com/us-news/2015/jun/27/beach-body-ready-america-weight-loss-ad-instagram

[10] https://dotsub.com/view/9d5cd50d-04b0-416e-8d79-0fc000f170c6/viewTranscript/eng

[11] https://ted.com/talks/rory_sutherland_life_lessons_from_an_ad_man

of marketing. We began by talking about grabbing attention. Advertising people often talk about AIDA, an acronym that you've seen means Attention, Interest, Desire, and Action. Advertising people use lots of acronyms and this one has gone in and out, and in again, of vogue. It stands for the process marketing people use to close the deal.

You've internalized the first lessons, that you must be objective and learn as much as possible about your customer (potential employer) and what she really needs, all the while thinking of yourself as a product. After you've figured out, from a truly objective point of view, what your prospective employer needs, and after you have attracted that person's attention with a well-written cover letter and resume that demonstrate you know her needs, you must create interest.

Interest can be created in many ways. Think about how product marketers attract your attention and then keep you interested to the point where you actually buy their product or service.

Humor

Humor certainly works, but it's tricky. What's funny to one person isn't necessarily funny to another, especially in a business setting. If you, fail, you look stupid and perhaps even offend the audience. The best bet is to avoid humor.

News

News creates interest, else why would so many people buy newspapers and watch news programs on the tube or the Internet. Why would we have such a fascination with new products? Why would we see the words "new" and "improved" all over packages (packaging, I might add, is a technique indispensable to marketing yourself.). Am I telling you to write "new" and "improved" in your cover letter? (Not unless you're applying for a creative job at an ad agency or design firm.)

So, how can you use news? Scan the headlines for news about the company you want to be employed by. For example, a job opens in the media relations department of a local hospital. That hospital recently began to use a new laser technique to treat brain tumors. Learn about this technique, then write a press release about this new treatment option. Show you know how to attract the attention of media.

Learn about the company you are interested in; this information could be invaluable when you get an interview with them. You could discuss events that occurred months ago or most recently. Not knowing about a major advancement by a company could put you at a disadvantage in an interview.

Sex

Can you use sex to create interest? Plenty of evidence exists to support the idea that a good-looking young man or woman can get a job because of her/his good looks (sex appeal). According to Business Insider, "Studies show that you're more likely to get hired *if you look well-groomed*, that *good-looking people make about 12% more money than less appealing folks*, and that *attractive real-estate brokers bring in more money than their less attractive peers*. Indeed, according to a…paper on *the 2018 congressional midterms*, more attractive candidates are more likely to get elected. Psychologists call it the 'beauty premium.' Essentially, *the income gap between attractive and unattractive people is comparable to the gap between genders or ethnicities.*[12]"

It's best to look your best, that's for sure, but your good looks will only set the stage for you. With attention to grooming and finding clothing that accentuate your assets while minimizing your flaws, you can look good. For instance, double-breasted suits, although quite fashionable, fit a thinner frame better. Tucks and gathers add unwanted breadth if you tend to be on the heavier side. Simple lines create the best appearance; wear colors that blend well with your natural color palette to enhance your appearance. Remember, you are the product and clothing is the packaging.

So, plan ahead; choose what you will be wearing to the interview days ahead of the interview. Pay attention to details—your clothes should be clean, ironed, and lint free; your shoes should be shined and the entire

---

[12] https://theladders.com/career-advice/11-scientific-reasons-why-attractive-people-are-more-successful-in-life

outfit coordinated. I had a very bright, personable student who made it to the final interview for a New York investment firm, a feat in itself. He performed extremely well in that final interview. He wore the starched white shirt, the red power tie, and the Brooks Brothers navy blue suit. However, he wore white socks. Those white socks cost him the interview and the job. Remember, the package must be fitting.

Study the Techniques That Create Interest

What techniques can you use to create interest? Emotional appeals create interest. So do references to well-known people, appeals to authority, testimonial (appealing to the person who's hiring through someone whose opinion they value, perhaps a good friend).

Suffice it to say, after you understand your customer's (hiring person's) needs, you must attract his or her attention, arouse his or her interest, and then close on him or her. We'll look at specific examples of this in the cover letter and resume.

Call-to-Action

If we agree that a marketing approach, heavy on promotion, is a good one, then a call-to-action is necessary after you've attracted attention, and created interest and desire. What's the use of going to all the trouble to attract attention to yourself, build interest and desire as a potential employee, and not following through with action? It's the close on the sale. "The offer expires today; call while supplies last; get yours now before they disappear; call our toll free number, you won't be disappointed, call before four o'clock and we'll send you a free alarm clock, and so on."

Am I telling you to use this kind of language to get a job? No, not really. Does a call-to-action work? Heck yes, or the nation's largest advertisers wouldn't use it. "Sports Illustrated" wouldn't use it so much on the late night infomercials. Is there a "respectable" call to action you can use? Most certainly.

If you watched *Dangerous Liaisons*, a movie of a few years back starring Michele Pfieffer, Glenn Close, and John Malkovich, you'll remember the monomaniacal need for the character Valmont (Malkovich) to close on his prey. He was single-minded and undeterred. He understood human nature and frailties. I would not want to have that character chasing someone I love!

You need a singleness of purpose that borders on Valmont's obsession to get the good job. That means calling for action, closing the sale. We'll discuss some of the ways in a later chapter.

Positioning Yourself

We're still talking about Promotion, the 4 Ps (plus two more Ps): Product, Price, Place, and Promotion; these are the "two more:" Positioning and Politics. (By the way, these four Ps are also known by these words: people, processes, performance, and programs.) One of the most brilliant marketing concepts ever came out of two guys named Ries and Trout in the 1970s in a book called, "Positioning.[13]" Essentially, they said that marketing is a battle for the mind of the customer and that a company (or person) must possess or create a uniqueness (a new position) so as to fill an opening which exists in the mind of a customer.

As examples, they used products such as Xerox, McDonald's, Scotch Tape, Kleenex, best known in the product category they occupy. Many of them are so well known that they have become a generic name for every product in their category.

In many instances, companies have become successful in positioning themselves because they were first in the category or first into the minds of the consumer. Domino's Pizza, Coke, Pampers, Tide, Ivory Soap are great examples. People can be "positioned," as well, especially if they are well known for "firsts" such as Neil Armstrong, Charles Lindberg, Amelia Earhart, and Sir Edmund Hillary. Other products have used positioning to give themselves a uniqueness are Avis (We're #2. We try harder), Volkswagen (Think Small), and 7Up (The Un-Cola).

You, too, have to be positioned, that is, known for something. You must differentiate yourself from the rest of the pack. Maybe it's that

---

[13] https://amazon.com/Positioning-Battle-Your-Al-Ries/dp/0071373586/ref=sr _1_2?dchild=1&keywords=positioning+trout&qid=1615053404&sr=8-2

you were a star lacrosse player, or a science wizard, maybe you wear a bow tie, or drive a Beetle. It's best to be separated from the mob by having some differentiating characteristic. Maybe you're a great writer, an organizer, or a budget manipulator. There has to be something you're best at, something you are even already known for. Think about it, and then take advantage of it by featuring it in your presentation/promotion.

You must make your differentiation immediately clear to your audience, the buyer, the hiring person, or company. Let's say that you're a finance major and you have studied all of the necessary finance courses, as well as statistics, data management, and some computer coding. Guess what, most of the other people applying for the finance position have the same background. Perhaps you went to Carnegie Mellon University and you've had two internships. Guess what, your competition may have gone to NYU and had two internships. It's awful. You still look alike.

What makes you different? The recruiter is really asking, "Why should I hire you and not the other person?" This is where you must differentiate, that is, position yourself.

You respond by telling a story: "When I was sixteen years old, my town in Taiwan was struck by an earthquake. Our home was destroyed and we were placed in a refugee camp. I studied hard and received a scholarship to one of the best universities in the world and then studied in America. I know what adversity means. I know how to overcome it. I have focus, a positive attitude, and an appreciation of life's good things. That earthquake helped to make me into a better person." How many people have lived through an earthquake and been relocated to a refugee camp to grow up, study, and be admitted to one of the best universities in the world? That's a differentiation and it works in a job search context.

Whatever uniqueness you claim, you must be able to relate it to the work the employer will want you to do. If you love sailing and you tell a story of having sailed across the English Channel as a teenager, by yourself, you must connect that to talents that the employer needs. You can say that you have always functioned well independently and that you created a plan for your crossing, that you made certain to have the right equipment, that you checked the weather, that you were focused, and that you got yourself into prime physical shape before you left. You can say that you worked with three friends to execute your crossing by keeping open communication with them during your trip. Then you can end by saying that you will bring these same qualities to work every day when hired: focus, planning, courage, commitment, and team work.

Branding

You have no doubt heard this term many times. But, what is a brand? According to Forbes magazine, the word "brand" has an interesting history: "Beginning in the later part of the 20th century, marketers began to grasp there was more to the perception of distinctive products and services than their names—something David Ogilvy described as "the intangible sum of a product's attributes." Marketers realized that they could create a specific perception in customers' minds concerning the qualities and attributes of each nongeneric product or service. They took to calling this perception "the brand."

"Put simply, your 'brand' is what your prospect thinks of when he or she hears your brand name. It's everything the public thinks it knows about your name brand offering—both factual (e.g., It comes in a robin's-egg-blue box), and emotional (e.g., It's romantic). Your brand name exists objectively; people can see it. It's fixed. But your brand exists only in someone's mind.[14]"

How does this relate to getting a job? Simply put, you will reflect an image from the sum of all that you communicate to another person. That will be your brand. The way you dress, the way you speak, the colors that you typically wear, the symbols associated with you, your words as found in social media, your education, all of this helps to create "The Brand Bob" or "The Brand Amanda" or "The Brand Xinru."

---

[14] https://forbes.com/sites/jerrymclaughlin/2011/12/21/what-is-a-brand-anyway/?sh=6e7f02b82a1b

Let's think about the brand "McDonald's" for a minute. You recognize it immediately because of the Golden Arches. You know Ronald McDonald. You connect red and yellow to the company. You've heard different slogans, such as, "I'm lovin' it." You probably also know the story of Ray Kroc who built the company into an international phenomenon.

The value of that brand in 2020 was $130 billion. That's just the brand, not the real estate, the buildings, or the burgers. Yes, a brand can be very valuable and very powerful. Yours can, too!

Think about your brand. What does it consist of? What colors do you wear? Do you have a flower in your hair or in your lapel? Do you say, "Yo, waz up" every morning to your colleagues? Or, do you wear a black t-shirt and blue jeans? Are you known to be fastidious and difficult to work with and have only the highest expectations (anyone thinking of the Steve Jobs brand)? Do you always send handwritten notes to people? Do you always sign your e-mails, "See you later, Alligator." Do you write conservative or progressive blog posts? Do you love to sky dive and use a picture of yourself at 20,000 ft. as your Facebook profile photo? Your brand starts to look like the sum of your public life.

A brand has also been called a "promise." It's an expectation. When you buy Polo, you can expect style every time. You can also expect a higher price. What is you promise? What can the buyer (employer) expect from you all the time? If you have no brand, you become generic. Do you want to be generic? I don't think so.

Key Concepts

People have little time and less attention.

Proven ways to attract attention include using: questions, quotes, stories, statistics, and disruptors.

We must use caution when disrupting for fear of amygdala hijack.

After we attract attention, we need to create interest and desire and use a call-to-action.

We must position (or differentiate) ourselves from the competition.

We can have a personal brand just as retail products are branded.

Take This Brand Quiz:

If I were an animal, what waould I be?_____

What car would I be?_____

What color represents me best?_____

What would my slogan be?_____

If I were a movie star, who would I be?_____

What song represents me?_____

How is my brand different from the competition?_____

What is my brand promise?_____

Answer These Questions

How am I positioned in the job marketplace?_____

What is my differentiation?_____

What is unique about me? _____

Why should someone hire me?_____

CHAPTER 6

It's Time to Act

If you attract attention to yourself, create interest and desire (let me find out more about this person), the last step is to ask for action. Ask for the sale. Don't wait for the goal to come to you. Go after your goals with a vengeance (and a nice attitude). You can take some tested approaches to this.

Ask for help

There really are no secrets in life. If you want to be a CEO, choose one you admire and copy him or her. If you want to write great ads, choose some great ads and copy them. If you want to be a researcher, snuggle up to a good researcher. In other words, get yourself near the kind of person you want to be, copy that person or ask her or him for help. Most people are flattered when asked for their expert opinions. I am. You can always ask Ed!

Let's say you've decided you want to work in health care marketing at St. Stanislaus Hospital in Yourtown but you're still in college, or you're working at a TV station. How do you pull this off if you're still in college? The easiest way is to register for classes taught by adjunct instructors; those are the part time teachers who work all day and teach at night for a small fee. They typically teach classes that are very practice-oriented and they are very connected in the world of work. If you can't find any of those, look for instructors who are active in the outside world (that is, off campus), either as consultants or board members. Check out the resumes of your teachers to look for their practical experiences (and possible connections).

In any event, the adjuncts are working out there, slugging it out every-day in the business world. Chances are they know the kinds of people you need to know at Yourtown Hospital. If you impress these instructors, they can serve as your cheerleaders or references. They can give you a head start on the rest of the pack.

Besides the meager money they make, adjuncts like to be admired. In their three-piece suits and power ties, they like to be perceived as people of authority and wisdom, decorated veterans of the employment wars. They like to tell stories. "Why, when I was your age ..." and "You wouldn't believe what happened to me at work today." Or "I once worked with this product, a rubber horseshoe." They are, if not the captains of industry, the busy privates and lieutenants, and they love to talk.

Ask these people to help you. Ask them for advice and for work experience in their shops. Every one of them has more work to do than people who are willing to help them complete that work. All of their contacts have more work to do, as well. Ask to meet with your adjunct, before class or at their office downtown in the early morning. (Forget after class. By that time, they've worked all day and want to go home.) Impress them in class with your enthusiasm and hard work. Attend regularly and participate in class. There is nothing worse for them than a class of sleepers. Find out what projects they are working on and volunteer to help.

This goes, too, for those of you who already have a job and are looking to change. I taught many students in the Heinz College of Carnegie Mellon University's Master of Public Management program. These were mostly people who were working full-time jobs all day and taking evening classes. They were able to network with each other and with me. In fact, I found them to be valuable connections, myself.

Volunteer to Help

That's right, volunteer. If you're just sitting around, why not volunteer your services. Guaranteed, if you came to me and asked if I needed any free help, I'd be very interested. Don't ask for money, but you may get some, anyway. Many businesses are budgeted for part-time help. Volunteer to help them or someone in their network whom they know to need help. If this experience is a good one, you'll learn more than you did in most of the classes you pay to take at college. And, most of these employers will find a way to pay you, anyway, out of a consulting line or somewhere.

Your enthusiasm, altruism, and willingness will give you opportunities that will provide you a little spending money and give you contacts and grist for your resume. It's also not unheard of that once these employers get to know you they'll consider you as a valid candidate when they have an opening, all because you volunteered to help them.

Be Persistent

You must persist at this, however. You must gently nudge and pursue these people. They are busy doing their jobs as well as the work of the person who may have resigned. You have to gather as much intelligence about their needs as you can, from them, and then convince them you can help. Nothing convinces these people like the word "free" coming from the mouth of a confident, hard-working, admiring student. Have I used such students? Absolutely. When I was a VP of Marketing for a large group of medical practices, I used two students (one graduate and one undergraduate) to work on marketing projects for a couple of medical practices. And, I paid them. They arranged grand openings, wrote promotional materials, and conceived advertising, among other things. I used another graduate student to develop a marketing plan, with my help, for a professional association of which I was a member. That experience effectively introduced him to a dozen more "movers and shakers," that is, people who offer employment or know where openings exist.

Most importantly, the experience gave them good stuff to put in their resumes under "Special Accomplishments." They look like real workers.

Take an Internship

Of course, the standard way to get experience is through the internship. Every year, thousands of students troop off to corporate America to perform their internship. For many of them it is a waste of time. And, it's their fault. They have failed to make themselves "indispensable". Or, they failed to make certain they would be performing meaningful work.

I think of interns as employees and, as such, will give them every opportunity to assume any responsibility. Why? Because there is always too much work to do and not enough people to do it. I'm as lazy as the next guy. If someone comes forward and convinces me she can accomplish a certain task, I'm a happy guy.

So, if you accept an internship (and you should only accept an internship where you know you'll have opportunities such as the ones I describe), you have to make them count. I have given interns very important projects to work on and when they succeeded have done everything I could to hire those people or to find them jobs.

A word of opinion: I tell my interns not to use the word "intern" on their resume. Unfortunately, in many people, it conjures up images of pimple-faced kids who get coffee and go to the copy machine. I'm telling you to appreciate the power of words, their denotation and connotation. Get some meaningful assignments and complete them. Do the work and you deserve to take credit for it, for having worked (not interned). If you intern with me, you work with me. I will verify that to anyone.

Assume a Posture

Ordinarily, the word "posturing" could be thought to be negative. But I say, posture away. Make yourself into a knowledgeable, powerful person. "Be all that you can be" (or pretend to be). Choose the right moment and the right project, pounce on it, and assume the posture of one who can accomplish the necessary ends. Say, "I'll handle this. Can we get together and discuss it. I have some questions I want to ask." (That's when you astound them by asking the objectives, targets, budget, etc.) And, don't blink. Puff yourself up, not into arrogance, but into the belief that you can handle the work. And, you can.

Nothing out there is so big or so important that one determined, focused person can't accomplish it with the help of others. Remember, Jimmy Carter, a peanut farmer from Georgia, became President of the United States, the most powerful person in the free world. Andrew Carnegie said he was a success because of the people who helped him. Even Mohammed Ali has admitted to "psyching himself up." Most of the leaders of corporate America would probably admit to some posturing.

One last word about posturing. I once worked at an independent video production company. It was a great company, staffed mostly by young, creative people, production assistants, gaffers, grips, gofers, lighting directors, set designers, videographers, producers, sales people, administrators, assistant directors, and directors. On every set, the director was in charge. I used to watch to see why everyone listened to the director but could find no tangible reason. Both assistant directors and directors were educated and experienced. But, the director was clearly in charge. Then it occurred to me that it was posturing. The director simply put herself in charge. She assumed a command presence, a director's presence, and called the shots, literally. That was that.

So I say to you, put your fear aside and take charge. You can do it. Remember, there's more work in any organization than there are people to do it. Crush your fear. It's the worst four-letter word in our vocabulary, far worse than the ones people rail about.

The stories that you will see below will show you how some friends of mine have taken temporary jobs, internships, and volunteer positions to get the jobs they wanted and to eventually reach their goals.

The "Ashley" Story

Ashley is a young lady of great ambition. She excelled in high school and won a scholarship to a prestigious small college where she graduated with honors in psychology. After her graduation, she enrolled immediately in graduate school to earn a master's in social work and found part time work as well as internships with social service agencies and hospitals. Upon completing her master's degree, she had several opportunities for full-time work and chose a small, for-profit company counseling youths and their families.

Not long after she joined the company, a manager's position opened. Because of her confidence in herself and despite her limited experience, Ashley applied for the manager's position. She wrote a compelling cover letter, fashioned a compelling resume, and adopted the posture of one who can manage the local office of a for-profit arm of the largest for-profit insurance company in the nation.

Did she posture? You bet she did. Was she frightened? You bet she was. Did she market herself to her superiors? She certainly did. Did she get the job, the corner office, the cell phone, the bonuses, the responsibility? Yes, she did. Can you do the same? Absolutely! Ashley would be the first person to tell you.

The "Rich" Story

Once upon a time when I was Director of Corporate Communications at a major teaching hospital, we needed a secretary. Who should apply for the position but a bright young guy named Rich who had completed a degree in Public Relations at a major city university. He had been, at the time, "temping," that is, working for agencies that specialize in temporary employment. He temped particularly in PR/Ad Agency/Marketing firms. His idea, obviously, was to be on the inside when jobs became available. He had temped at our hospital, and in our office, and had impressed everyone. When the time came that we needed help, we were interested in him and we hired him.

Rich subscribed to the principles in this book. He knew how to make himself indispensable. He was ambitious and likeable. He asked the important questions. In addition, he had tremendous computer and organizational skills. He volunteered regularly for extra work and he managed the work strategically, that is, he developed plans. Before he left us, he had been promoted three or four times, he had managed advertising campaigns, he had interacted at the highest levels of the organization, and he had built a fat resume of accomplishments.

Rich left us to move to a warmer part of the country, landed a good job in a hospital and then went to work as a group account manager at a major ad agency in the city. Now, of course, he owns his own agency. He knows what he wants, he's focused, and he is confident.

The "Shelly" Story

Shelly was a woman I knew from the university. She was a very bright, engaging, and an enthusiastic young woman who happened to be a special education major. Because she was pretty, dynamic, and friendly (and because there was a demand for special education teachers) she found a job quickly after graduating from college. To help pay her way through graduate school, she accepted work as a temp during the summer months. Her graduate work was in human resource management and she always asked for temporary assignments in the human resource offices of major corporations. Before long, she became indispensable to a major corporation in Dallas and they offered her a full-time position in the HR office (which she accepted with the promise that the company would pay for her master's degree). Today she is a Vice President of Human Resources with another major company in Houston.

Shelly was attractive, persistent, friendly and willing to do the extra work no one else wanted to do. She was enthusiastic and had a great sense of humor.

Why have I repeated "sense of humor?" Because it is important to have balance in your life, both professional and personal. If you think being a success is the result of 16-hour days of intensity and irritation, you're wrong. For you to be a success, you must balance hard work with hard fun. You must balance your strategic mind with your creative mind. Lighten up and move up!

The "Linn" Story

Linn was a woman who married, had two children and decided to go for a master's in communication. A persistent individual, she graduated with honors in communication and immediately took a job with a large corporation. She couldn't connect right away in the communication department so she took a job in security. In the meantime, she didn't give up her focus. She volunteered at a public television station in the community affairs department and networked by going to meetings of professional societies and asking for "informational interviews." In effect, she worked two jobs, one as a full-time security person and the other as a full-time job seeker.

Through her networking, Linn met a person who worked in my department and impressed him as mature, intelligent, motivated, and personable. When she left his office, he practically ran down the hall to tell me about her, saying, "You've got to hire this person before someone else does." We didn't have an immediate opening but a few months later, as luck would have it, someone decided to leave our department. We interviewed Linn and others. She was very impressive and her work as a security guard piqued my curiosity. Her life was a story of drive and desire and we hired her. My colleague was right. Linn was, and still is, exactly the kind of employee anyone would want. Today she is a VP at a bank.

Key Concepts

Ask for help; people will help you.

Be persistent; it pays off.

Do something. Volunteer. Take an unpaid internship. Become indispensable to someone or some company.

Assume a power posture. Show command presence. If you can't, fake it till you make it.

Answer These Questions

Who are the people I can approach and ask for help?_____

Where can I volunteer so as to meet the right people?_____

What internships are available?_____

Do I look confident?_____

Do I hold myself erect, shoulders back, chin level, making eye contact?

_____

Do I have a command posture?_____

Would people follow me?_____

CHAPTER 7

Promotional Materials

Everything You Write Must Be Interesting and Offer Benefits, Even Your Resume

So, you've searched your soul to determine exactly the kind of job you want, you've surfed the Internet, you've connected with adjunct teachers and their networks, you've volunteered at the company where you'd really like to make your fortune, you've written the most engaging cover letter ever. Now you need the killer resume.

Your Resume—One Fundamental

If you accept the notions already discussed herein—you are marketing yourself, you must be objective, you need to differentiate yourself—you'll accept this important fundamental: your resume is a piece of writing, words on a piece of paper. For that reason, your resume needs to be interesting to read, no different than any other interesting reading, newspaper, novel, whatever. Is this what many others tell you? Au contraire. They tell you to be boring. The more boring the better. Deadly boring. Science abstract boring. Legal jargon boring.

The best way to bore your reader is with obsessive talk about yourself. Obviously, your resume is a record of your work and accomplishments. However, I suggest you write it in such a way as if you were writing about another person, that is, telling a compelling story about another person.

When you write about that person, write with vivid, concrete, active language. Avoid abstraction at all costs. The very worst abstractions are called, "Objective" statements. As in, "I want to work for a growing company where I can make a commitment, a contribution and pursue a career." And what do many others tell you? Begin your resume with an abstraction!

You should begin your resume, not with a boring "Objective," but with the most engaging, attention-grabbing statement in your arsenal, that is, your very best "Special Accomplishment," the only thing about which you are most proud, and, more importantly, the one thing which will connect with the reader's needs. You must use words that suggest benefits to the reader. You must choose those words carefully because words have power. Ask yourself this question: what does the hiring manager want? Then answer that question in your summary.

The Useless Career Objective

Do you have the word "Objective" written at the top of your resume? If you do, you're like 50 percent of all job seekers, particularly recent college graduate job seekers. You undoubtedly have a boring resume as well. I'll bet you have "References available upon request" typed in the center bottom of your one-page boring resume. If you have either or both of these two items on your resume, tear it up and start over again. You are being boring and trite.

When you begin with your objective, you are violating the first rule: focus on the audience and its needs, not your own. Start with a suggestion of the benefits you will bring to the job. Go back and look at the benefits we discussed: maturity, teamwork, and experience. Discuss those first! Impress the reader right at the outset.

Another Fundamental

You typed your resume on your computer, right? Or you had your girlfriend or computer geek boyfriend do it for you since he knew how to access the different "Word" typefaces. You then walked this resume into a print shop, probably Kinko's, and paid to have fifty or a hundred copies printed. Right? Unless you had someone finance your resume printing (mothers and fathers don't count), you paid to print the thing. The bottom line for those who still send a hard copy is you paid for the resume. If it represents your work life to date, if you slaved over the writing of it, if you paid 50 bucks for copies, why would you let someone else tell you how to write it? Another fundamental is Write Your Own Resume.

Don't let someone who has little experience in the world of work tell you how to do it.

How Long Should It Be?

I am ever amazed at my students when I give them a writing assignment. They always ask, "How long should it be?" I always baffle them by replying "Two and a half feet". The correct answer is: Your resume needs to be as long as it is to do what it has to do and still be interesting. That long and no longer.

Some uninformed people will tell you that your resume should never be more than one page long. It's amazing. Saying that your resume should be only one page is as arbitrary as saying your resume should always be ten pages. Where did they get this number? Mostly people say this to you because they don't want to deal with reading more pages.

A resume needs to be as long as it is interesting. That means it must be written very carefully with a full understanding of how people read and what interests them.

I say, again, your resume should be as long as is necessary to tell a good story about you. Is this good advice in an electronic age? Definitely. Good writing is good writing, whether it's on a monitor or in the hands. Even if it's sent by e-mail, it will probably be converted to paper.

Write an interesting summary of your life. Use vivid language and measurable examples. Become a human being right in front of your reading audience, not a cardboard cut-out. Not a carbon copy of every other resume out there. By all means, do not use a format. You should even view my format with skepticism. If tomorrow everyone starts using the Ed Barr Format, then you will be nondifferentiating. You must show how you differ from the crowd of people who essentially have the same education and experience that you have.

Your Resume, You Own It

The first thing on your resume is your name. Nothing fancy. First name, middle initial, and last name, followed by your address, phone number, and e-mail address. Listen carefully to this advice: NO Temporary

Addresses, NO temporary phone numbers, NO post office boxes, NO pager numbers, NOTHING that suggests that you are in transit or in any way unstable. Put this information in the center of your resume. Don't make the reader jump from the left hand corner to the right hand corner to know these important facts about yourself. If you are applying to an American company and you come from another country and have a name that an American will have trouble saying, use an English name.

The Five Critical Parts of Your Resume

Executive Summary (or Profile)

What you need is a "grabber" statement, something that will impress them right off the bat, something that says, this candidate knows what needs to be done in an office like ours. What is that magic statement? It's your "Executive Summary." Isn't that a great title?! It means you are calling the reader an executive. Who doesn't want to be referred to as an executive? In this summary, you must say the things that match the readers' needs. We talked about them earlier. They want teamwork, experience, maturity, ethics, experience, results, and other such characteristics. If that's what they want, you must tell them that's what you have.

> *Ed Barr Executive Summary: Deeply experienced former chief marketing officer with measurable accomplishments, high energy, and proven success with diverse teams around the world. Innovative problem-solver, award winning CMU professor, and former coach of champion wrestling and football teams.*

Now, you will notice right away that I talked about football and wrestling in my marketing resume. Why did I do that? Well, for several reasons. First, it creates cognitive dissonance and the reader notices it and will remember it (it sits in one of the serial positions, last). Second, it differentiates me from all other candidates. Third, it shows that I can lead teams, manage them, motivate them, and create winners. Not bad characteristics for a future marketing executive, right?

People who read resumes read them from the top down. You need to grab them right away since they only spend a few seconds with your resume. Write something that appeals to them and rattles them a little. Then, keep their attention as you move to the next important section of your resume, which, by the way, isn't your education. Everyone applying for the job you want has an education. You need to keep showing how you will benefit the buyer, the recruiter, and the company. Your record of accomplishments shows that. We all know that education isn't the critical test, with the exception of a few professions; think brain surgeon. (In many ways, having no education is better. It is certainly a differentiator for most professional jobs and it suggests that you have the kind of intelligence that is innate. But, I don't suggest that you drop out of school. The Steve Jobs of the world are few and far between.)

Special Accomplishments—Right Up Front

The person reading your resume is selfish. She wants to know what you can do for her. It's that simple. This is not a person who doesn't have anything better to do so has decided to spend the weekend reading a hundred or so cover letters and resumes.

What does this mean to you? It means "cut to the chase." Give this person some immediate reason to be interested in you and to continue reading. Put one of your proudest moments right up front, your "Special Accomplishments," things you have done in your past which are measurable and impressive and lead a list of other measurable and impressive accomplishments.

At this point, my students always respond (typically in chorus), "But I don't have any special accomplishments." And I say, "Phoooie." Of course you have accomplishments.

For instance, I once had a CEO from AT&T tell me he would always interview an Eagle Scout. We were both on the local board of the Boy Scouts and understood the difficulty of rising to the rank of Eagle Scout (by the way, I never became more than a tenderfoot; it's a long story). Many corporate leaders volunteer for community boards. You never know when your audience is one of those people.

I always interview a Viet Nam, or any other, vet. In my estimation, the men and women who defended this country or served to protect it deserve consideration. You may not have been in the armed services, but you may have been in a fraternity or sorority. You never know when the person reading your resume has decided he will always interview someone because he's a fraternity brother or she's a sorority sister. Others might always interview a football player or Key Club officer. You never know.

The catch is to make your experience as fraternity member or officer (or wrestling coach) translate into a benefit to the person reading your resume. As always, it depends upon how you say it. Saying the best thing poorly can shortchange you.

Accentuate the Positive

I tell students to "elaborate," accentuate the positive, eliminate the negative (unless it can serve to generate positive attention). I never tell anyone to lie (despite the fact that it's estimated that nearly "90 percent of the time people lie on their resumes," this according to Patricia Gillette, a San Francisco lawyer, as quoted in "Maxim" magazine[1]). And, dishonesty is a very difficult thing to prove. For instance, if you take samples of work (brochures, news placements, writing, design), to an interview, who's to prove you didn't actually do the work, especially in the "team" context where everybody has some involvement in the work. However, I advise against any dishonesty on resumes. Dishonesty has a way of catching up with people and when it does you will lose your job and your reputation. It's not worth it.

As long as we're talking about taking things into an interview, I give you this advice—don't drag a fat portfolio to your meeting. Select a couple pieces that best represent your work, or even what you believe to be good work, and show them in that context. I appreciate knowing what a candidate thinks is good work. I then know if his judgment and values fit with the organization. For instance, I've interviewed writers and always ask them to tell me what they think is a great piece of writing.

I once had an older candidate bring a thick, sloppy portfolio stuffed with just about every article and brochure he had ever written. The newspaper pages were yellowed, gnarled, and a bad reflection on him (to say nothing of emphasizing just how old and out of touch he was).

---

[1] https://nelliganlaw.ca/e/pdf/Dont_Hire_a_Liar.pdf

Bring one glamour piece and let that speak to your taste, judgment, and style. The more expensive the better. Nobody wants cheap, even if that's all they can afford.

List Your Special Accomplishments Proudly

Whatever they are, they must be translated in concrete, specific, and measureable terms. If you coordinated the Phoota Ooota Koota Spring Fraternity Social, you need to report this accomplishment as an operational and financial one. For instance, you might say, "Coordinated the 1998 Phoota Ooota Kooda Spring Social by managing committee of six and $3000 budget for promotion, entertainment, site, food, security. Realized $6000 profit for use in scholarship fund." Pretty darn impressive business accomplishment! It's measureable and proves team work, responsibility, stewardship, and energy.

All of a sudden what you considered a mere pedestrian event, a fraternity social where you may have been out of control and wearing a lampshade on your head, is translated into a business accomplishment. Instead, people use the most boring words and examples, almost as if they're begging to say, I never did anything!

I never cease to be amazed at the effect of words and people's ignorance of their effect. For instance, what does the word "McDonald's" conjure in your mind? You might say, "Golden Arches," "Ronald McDonald," "Quarter Pounder." To me, the word means, "bad tasting, fast food, slick promotions and all the evils of a fast-paced, society of consumption."

Maybe I'm alone in that assessment, maybe not. In any event, you take a chance anytime you use the word "McDonald's" or Dress Barn, or Peter's Pub, or any word which suggests temporary, semiskilled labor (unless, of course, you're looking to make McDonald's a career).

Most student resumes I have reviewed use McDonald's, Dress Barn, and Vinnie's Video Shop without a second thought as to what images those words conjure in the minds of a reader.

I say, never use words like those when you can say differently, and to greater effect, something else. Remember, this is your resume. You wrote it and paid to have it printed. Those are your stamps on the envelope you also paid for. You can say it any way you want.

So, why say, for instance, "McDonald's—summers 1996 to 1998," when you can say, "Special Accomplishment—Raised $12,000 for my education by working three summers" (or whatever amount you raised). Seriously, doesn't that sound more impressive and related to the business world? All I can imagine in the word "McDonald's" is an unhappy, dissatisfied, disgruntled, uniformed, kid in a greasy hat asking me if I want fries with my shake.

Use the Word "Intern" Advisably

Every word you use has power. It has a connotation and a denotation. Even before Monica Lewinsky the term "intern" brought to mind someone wondering around the hallways of a corporation trying to find the rest room. I say, don't use the word "intern." Instead, use the name of the place where you worked (unless, of course, you interned at McDonald's). Use the name of the place where you worked because if you were anything more than a slug you did work there—you just weren't paid (unless it was a paid internship).

Come to work with me, or for an "enlightened" employer like me. I'll give you important assignments and allow you to experience success and failure. Then later I'll serve as your reference and tell everyone about your good work. I've already done it for many "interns" and so have many of my colleagues. Before accepting a position as an intern, make certain you will be doing meaningful work, interacting in the department, and learning. You might even ask for a job description. Above all, don't accept being treated like a go-fer.

Avoid Detailed Dates

Every resume of every young person begins with the ever-deadly Objective followed closely by an Education and then Employment History (since that's what most placement counselors tell them to begin with). This Employment History, an unimpressive list of McDonald's Restaurants and Dress Barns, is preceded by dates. The effect looks something like this:

A Bad Resume

Andy Jobseeker

4511 Springwood Road

Yourtown, PA 12602

(814) 948-1234 temporary

(412) 328-1234 parents

(814) 948-1111 Pager Number (enter #152, then 963)

Career Objective -   To find employment where I can use the skills I learned in college to help the less fortunate find peace in their lifetimes

Employment History

  – Food Service Specialist, Blu's Burgers, Yourtown, PA

  6-6-20 to 8-31-20

  – Intern, PR Department, Holy Gospel Hospital, Yourtown, PA

  1-25-20 to 5-5-20

  – Life Guard, Gentry Country Club, Yourtown, PA

  6-5-15 to 8-29-18

  – Babysitter, Yourtown, PA   5-31-15 to 9-1-18

Education

  BA, Business Administration, Upland University, Baltimore, MD (expected 2021)

Other Experiences

  Secretary of Phoota Ooota Kooda International Fraternity, Upland Chapter
  Member - Drama Club of Upland
  Cast of 'Romeo and Juliet' played Mercutio

References available upon request

Here, in plain view, is your admission that you've never done anything that you find important or interesting, and you've never done it for more than the summer months. In other words, you paint yourself as an ineffective dolt. You are a victim of your own interpretation of yourself. You have "dumbed yourself down" and, thereby, make it very easy to put your resume quickly into the rejects' pile. You have accentuated the mediocre, undersold yourself. Your only success was to make certain we could find you for your rejection letter. (By the way, any time you apply for a job and don't hear from someone within two weeks by telephone, you can pretty much forget it. If you receive a letter in the mail, especially one with a mailing label, throw it away, unopened, or mark it "return to sender." I can guarantee there's a form rejection inside.)

Special Accomplishments—Yet Again

Almost no one cares where you went to college. Sad but true. Sure, some colleges have a bigger brand name than others. Harvard has the distinction of having been the first university in America. What was the second? Few people know. (William and Mary, surprised?) All the Ivy League schools have a certain cache. Even Carnegie Mellon has some brand power, mostly in the United States. Also sad but true is the reality that your undergraduate training is almost no indication of how well you will do at your job. Plenty of Ivy League grads are no farther ahead of small college grads, or high school grads, in the world of work. Talent is no predictor of success. Nothing is as wasted in this world as talent. Persistence is more important. Show persistence in your resume. Save your college credentials for later in the resume.

Persistence can be demonstrated by your special accomplishments, your measureable accomplishments. You supervised 25 children, ages 5 to 17 for two weeks 24 hours per day at summer Heart Camp in Oshkosh. All attendees were former open-heart surgery or heart transplant patients. You scheduled all activities, physical, educational, and counseling. Your performance was rated 9.1 on a 10-point scale. Or, you reduced theft at Dress Barn by 27 percent by implementing "Employee

Watch and Incentive" program. You surpassed sales quota by 11 percent at Vinnie's Video in March 2018. You increased membership at Phoota Ooota Kooda fraternity by 33 percent over the previous pledge period by instituting an on-campus promotional strategy. You bowled a 300 game. (Don't smirk. It takes a lot of practice, patience, and talent to bowl a 300 game.) In any event, you have turned your experiences into the language of the reader and have suggested benefits and reasons for them to consider buying your services (even though you worked at Dress Barn and Vinnie's Video).

Work Experience

List the places where you worked, unless it was McDonald's. Don't list that. Remember: translate it as working three summers to earn $12,000 for your education.

Your responsibility to yourself is to get that interview. Seriously, your obligation to yourself, and to your future employer, is to have them see you and question you face to face. Very few jobs are awarded simply on the view of a resume.

Should you put dates? Only if it helps you. I worked at one place for 14 years after having had a series of 2-year jobs. (I was restless and confused. It happens.) The 14 years demonstrated real stability after the jumping around. List the dates when they can help you. I do NOT put years of graduation or years that would date me. Age discrimination is alive and well, along with every other type of discrimination, in the United States.

As I said, if I'm hiring you, I'm interested in what you have achieved, specifically and measurably, whether it was in high school, college, the armed forces, at a part time job, whatever. How much responsibility did you have and how did you handle it? Most employers want a self-starting, self-motivated, achiever. They don't want to hire someone and then have to discipline or fire that person. It's too much trouble. Employers must create job descriptions, get them improved, get a position budgeted, advertise the position, collect resumes and cover letters, read them, set appointments for interviews, interview, bring some candidates back for second interviews, third interviews, negotiate offers, allow the chosen candidate to give a two-week notice and finally start the new job. That takes much time and many resources. Then, too, it's nearly impossible to fire someone these days, anyway, without first chances, second chances, corrective action plans, Employee assistance programs (EAPs), paper trails, exhaustion, sinking morale. Make me confident that you're the right person. So, show me in measurable language your previous accomplishments.

Education

Is a college education important? Yes. By all means, state the name of your alma mater. Who knows, maybe the interviewer went there. Seriously, it's true that if you don't have the degree you won't get the good job. The lack of a four-year education eliminates a lot of good people. The diploma is a ticket to the dance. Crashing the party is harder and harder, although some brave souls have accomplished it and have emerged financially more successful than the "educated" (do the names Bill Gates and Steve Jobs ring any bells?).

A college degree does not predict success. A Bachelor's degree these days is as easy to get as a high school diploma, particularly in the humanities (it's a little harder to fake it in the sciences).

Special Interests

I once interviewed a young woman who listed "Professional Football" as a special interest. It attracted my attention and I asked her what she meant by it. She said, "Oh, I just put that there because my boyfriend told me it would get your attention." She was right, it did, but I didn't hire her. She was flat, uninteresting, and unmotivated. She got in the door but she couldn't follow through. I would have preferred the professional football to have been her idea. It would have shown some creativity.

Are you a parachutist? List it. Are you a tri-athlete? List it. Do you breed dogs? List it. The idea of a resume and cover letter is to present you, as much as possible, in three dimension since you can't do it yourself.

I want to see you in my mind's eye, rock climbing, swimming the Hudson Bay, sitting at a magnifying glass tying flies, doing the thing that makes you a human being.

My resume says that I was a football and wrestling coach. I could have put that in the special interests place on my resume, but I chose instead to put it in the executive summary because I knew it would attract attention, differentiate me, and disrupt anyone reading a resume about a chief marketing officer candidate.

Your resume should create a hologram of you, making you appear before my eyes in my office. Tall order? You bet! Would you rather be interesting or boring? Maybe if you want to be an actuary or a banker you should be boring, but I doubt it. In any event, it's your choice.

A story about Interests. A Managing Director at a large international bank told me that when he receives a resume he goes right to the bottom. Yes, right to the bottom where he'll find their interests. Why does he do that? He said, "At this level the candidates are all the same. They all have the same coursework in college, the same degrees, and the same internships and experience. I want to find out what makes one different from the other. I want to get a peek behind the scenes at a human. The interests give just that, a peek. Otherwise, they are one-dimensional words on a piece of paper, not yet people."

Make your resume tell your story. We are born storytellers and we live our lives inside stories.

Reasons to Include References

Why would you not include references? My older students tell me they don't want their bosses to know they're looking for another job, that someone might call one of their in-company references, or the boss herself. To this I say, "Phooie." No one can fire you for looking at other opportunities. If anything, passing your resume to a few people should signal your boss to make things better or risk losing you. Besides, if you're an older employee or another protected category, you're well protected against discrimination.

Why should you include your references? Because you need all the help you can get in this ever more crowded job market. This is a version of the old marketing saying, "The more you tell, the more you sell." If you get only one shot at promoting yourself, why not use all the ammunition at your disposal? Suppose you use me as a reference and suppose one of my fraternity brothers receives your resume. Right, you've got an automatic connection you would not otherwise have. It could be my business associate or my neighbor. What does it cost you to include a separate page of references—nothing—or to save a little space at the bottom for a name or two? Do it. Include them. If nothing else, it will fill out your direct mail package. Remember, direct mail technique calls for more than one item in that envelope.

Things not to do (unless you're after a graphic design job)

Do NOT use an oversized piece of paper.
Do NOT use weirdly colored paper. White and buff will do nicely.
Do NOT use calligraphy or weird typefaces.
Do NOT use a color of ink other than black.

A Good Resume

So, what makes a good resume? Good writing, good layout, good results. A good resume is easy to handle, easy to read, and demonstrates results while projecting a three-dimensional image of its owner, an image which creates a dynamic, interesting individual—both personally and professionally.

The development of such a resume is not, as they say, rocket science, but it does require thought and work. It is, however, good, common sense. The reason no one uses common sense in creating a resume is that we are told that the resume must fit a prescribed format and set of rules. Your resume will look like a resume but with a little care and common sense it doesn't have to be boring, ineffective and, worst of all, overlooked.

Following is a sample of a good resume. Check it out.

A Sample Resume

Eric Jobman
1313 Mockingbird Lane
Yourtown, NY 12345
(312) 987-6543 (H)
(312) 789-6543 (W)
E-Mail ejobman@marketman.com

Executive Summary – *Deeply experienced marketing professional with measurable accomplishments, high energy, and proven success with diverse teams. Innovative problem-solver, award winning CMU professor, and former coach of champion wrestling and football teams, a winner who knows how to plan, execute, and follow through.*

Special Career Accomplishments

- *Developed network-wide and individual practice marketing plans for 80 practice medical practice network targeted to increase enrollment by 15% in the first year.*
- *Developed and implemented customer service strategies to include "Customer Service Standards" in-service training to 245 staff.*
- *Developed advertising campaign for medical practice network targeted to produce 12,000 telephone responses to practice hotline.*
- *Developed computer system in project management, to include $400,000 cost savings and 10% complaint reduction.*
- *Developed home page designed to generate 500 "hits" per day.*
- *Created pro-active crisis communication plans for three hospital crisis scenarios.*
- *Increased staff and physician community involvement by 22% in first year.*
- *Coached city championship football team and state champion wrestler.*

Work Experience

2015–Present	*Chief Marketing Officer, Illustrious University*
2010–2015	*Vice President, Marketing - Doctors Network of Yourtown*

2015–2010   Director of Communications - Yourtown Hospital
EDUCATION   University of Pennsylvania, MBA
*   Cornell University, BS*

Special Interests

— *Member - Board of Trustees - Renewit, Inc., Community corrections facility, Yourtown, NY - responsible for ad-hoc marketing committee and planning for marketing of resource management software to corrections industry*
— *Tutor Trainer - Yourtown Literacy Initiative - Trained over 75 tutors to work with illiterate*
— *Music Teacher - Youth Opportunities, Community agency for underprivileged children, Yourtown, NY - taught seven children basic guitar*
— *Member – America Marketing Association*
— *Member - Yourtown Television and Radio Club*

But, you'll say, you do not have twenty years of great accomplishments to list. And to that I say, You're not listening. Everyone has an interesting life in some way. Even you! Actually, I left out a major portion of my work history, which is another way of saying, "It's your life; you get to say what you want to say to your very best advantage." You want the interview. After you get it, you can fill in any gaps that interest the recruiter.

Key Concepts

Words have power.

Your resume must tell a story.

Your story must show the readers potential benefits to them.

People read resumes from the top down; you must put the most critical information at the top.

Your resume must differentiate you.

Having an education probably does not differentiate you these days; top schools will, however.

You have had special accomplishments in your life; show them.

Be certain that you show measureable accomplishments. Four will do.

Show work experience, even if it was nonpaid.

Include your references. Why wouldn't you?

Answer These Questions

What can I say about myself in the first sentences, the Executive Summary, that will show the readers how I will benefit them?_____

_____

What are my special, measureable accomplishments?_____

Does my resume tell a story?_____

How do I make the readers want to meet me?_____

CHAPTER 8

Getting Yourself Better Known

So, we've discussed a lot about marketing but still haven't talked about how you can make a name for yourself so that employers and recruiters seek you out, instead of you having to look for them. This takes planning and energy, but you are up for it, and you're doing a lot of it already, as in social media. But, let's defer that for a moment and talk about networking.

Network or Not Work, You Decide

Few people like to do it, but most people realize the importance of networking. We are a social species, introverts, or extroverts. We have been able to build towering cities and civilizations because of our social nature. We live in a web or connections—family, relatives, friends, colleagues, and random others. We can find help from all of these people. But, we need to ask. We need to expand our webs by asking each one to connect us to three more, or four more, or many, many more. We need to make the connections and keep them by providing something of value. We want these connections to know, like, and trust us. We want to offer a valuable service, ultimately. This is two-way conversation.

How Do You Network?

You need not dread networking. Like everything else, you need a plan. You need objectives, strategies, and actions.

When you set out to network, you need to identify the kinds of people you want to connect with and write some measureable objectives. For instance, you might say, "I will identify 25 people in my discipline and connect with them within 30 days."

But, how does a person network? First, you begin with the low hanging fruit. Ask your parents, your siblings, your neighbors, your friends, your teachers about the people they know. Ask them to introduce you to some of their friends and associates who can help you. Join and use LinkedIn (more on this later). If you are attending a college or have graduated, ask the alumni office to share with you the names and e-mail addresses of the alumni who match your career choice. Write to these people. Ask them for an informational interview or ask them to connect you to three other people you should know. Build a pyramid, such as many churches do for fundraising. You stand at the top of the pyramid. You are given names by three people; they stand just under you. Those three people give you three more and on and on. Now you have nine people. Those nine give you three names each. Soon you have a huge pyramid of potential contacts (or donors for the church).

Pay attention to the way you approach these people. They are busy and distracted. They probably don't know you. They have other things on their minds. You must attract their attention and give them some reason for wanting to connect with or talk with you. This is all based in self-interest. Your e-mail or letter needs to reflect that. Here's a sample e-mail from a person looking for a connection.

All right, you wrote a great message and your target has accepted the invitation for a coffee chat. Now what do you do?

Be Interested, Not Interesting

The best way to blow this opportunity is to go to your meeting and talk about yourself for the allotted 15 minutes. The best way to have a great meeting and to get the most from that connection is to ask questions and let your company do the talking. We all like to talk about ourselves because, as I have said, we are all motivated by self-interest. So, keep the conversation going by asking questions. Ask these:

- To what do you attribute your career success?
- What is the most valuable piece of advice anyone has ever given you?

A Sample E-Mail

To: Potential connection

From: You

Subject: You have helped so many people

Body: Your friend, I'm a Buddy, suggested that I write to you. She told me of the many wonderful things you have done to help others, including your selfless work with the American Cancer Society. She said that you have often connected to people who are beginning their careers. You have such a respected place in this community and in your profession that I would be honored if you would allow me to connect with you on LinkedIn. I know you review these requests carefully so I will tell you that I am attending Illustrious University and majoring in marketing with a 3.9 GPA. I have had two great internships with ABZ and XYT companies.

I would love to hear how you got your start in this career and what recommendations you would make to a rookie like me. I know how extremely busy you are, but if you would meet with me for fifteen minutes, perhaps for a cup of coffee I have just three questions I'd like to ask you.

If you are too busy right now, I certainly understand. However, if you can meet briefly with me, I'll buy the coffee and meet you at your favorite coffee shop. Regardless, I admire all that you have done in your career as reflected on LinkedIn and I thank you for your attention to this message. I will call your office within the week to make an appointment if you are agreeable.

- What process did you use when you were in my position to get the job you wanted?
- Are you willing to give me the names of three people whom I can contact for a coffee chat?

The best thing to do is to send your coffee mate the questions you'd like to cover *before* you meet. This is not just respectful but it shows the person that you do not meet to waste her time.

Be early for the meeting. Dress appropriately, business casual. Be familiar with the person by looking on line for photos of her. You might also send a photo of yourself and say, "I have blonde hair, stand five foot ten and I'll be wearing a navy blue sports coat." As the meeting progresses, after you have had your coffee (which you have paid for), watch the time. Typically, your guest will spend more than 15 minutes with you, being caught up in telling her stories and impressing you. It's human nature. And, be respectful of their time. When they say they must leave, be gracious.

After the meeting, send a quick e-mail. Don't forget to mention something important she said as being important to you. If possible, send her something, such as a link to an article that might interest her, as an act of generosity and gratitude.

How important is networking? Look at this from "topresume," an online resume service,

> *60 percent of jobs are found through networking—not online. While websites like Glassdoor and ZipRecruiter are certainly helpful tools for your job search, it's important to look beyond these online job boards. A majority of job postings are not available online, with 60 percent of jobs being found through networking instead.*
>
> *What does that mean for you as the job seeker? Simple: You need to start networking. A good strategy is to go directly to the website of the companies that you're targeting, do a little digging, and pinpoint a few decision makers. Don't go too high up the ladder and try to connect with the C-level team to ask about available job positions—they likely won't reply. Instead, target those with titles like Director and Manager. They are often the ones who'll be in charge of making hiring decisions.*
>
> *Connect with those professionals on LinkedIn and let them know that you're interested in their company. Either through email or a face-to-face informational interview, communicate why you would love to work there and your enthusiasm for the industry itself.* [1]

---

[1] https://topresume.com/career-advice/7-top-job-search-statistics#:~:text=60%20 percent%20of%20jobs%20are%20found%20through%20networking%20 %E2%80%94%20not%20online&text=A%20majority%20of%20job%20 postings,being%20found%20through%20networking%20instead.

By the way, the best questions to ask are: what, why, and how questions. If you ask who, when, and where questions you're likely to get one-word responses. Those make even a 15 minutes session very painful.

Promoting Yourself on the Internet

Nearly 300 million people in the United States use the Internet. Something like 260 million people are active mobile Internet users. Just under 250 million people are active social media users. And, over 230 million people are active mobile social media users.[2] Do you use Facebook? Who doesn't? Are you on Instagram? TikTok? WeChat? Others? You need to be there but you need to be there advancing your brand image, not tarnishing it.

Use LinkedIn

If you are not on LinkedIn, you are truly wasting a golden opportunity to connect to thousands of people, many who can help you. LinkedIn, as we know, has millions of professionals registered. If you spend some time on this site, you will find a ton of information, as well as insightful posts from people who are practicing a form of B2B marketing (business-to-business). It's important that you have two things: a great profile statement and some references from others.

What do job sites say about LinkedIn? Listen to this:

77 percent of recruiters rely on LinkedIn. While LinkedIn is a powerful job-search tool, it is also a way for recruiters to reach out to prospective candidates about job opportunities. In fact, LinkedIn remains the most-used channel for recruitment efforts. This means that if you don't have a LinkedIn profile, or you haven't touched your profile in a while, you are missing out on ample job opportunities. The key to getting noticed by recruiters on LinkedIn? Optimize your profile with your experiences and skills using appropriate keywords,

---

[2] https://statista.com/statistics/1044012/usa-digital-platform-audience/

write a captivating profile summary, interact with other users, share important articles or findings about your industry, and stay active on the site.[3]

Before you write your LinkedIn profile statement, think carefully about the words you will use. Think, not about the words that you like, but about the needs of the people who will review your statement. Think of the one word that differentiates you and offers a benefit.

Own a Word?

Optimize your profile! In this age of oversaturated media and audiences, you need to own one word. Listen to this from Daniel Pink, author and teacher,

"I was thinking about the business implications of the Obama juggernaut the other day when a friend said to me," "I can't think of the word 'hope' any more without thinking of the guy." " Something about that comment stuck in my head. Then this afternoon, I was going through some piles of clippings and ran across a column by Maurice Saatchi *in which he lays out his theory of "one-word equity":*

"What I am describing here is a new business model for marketing, appropriate to the digital age. In this model, companies compete for global ownership of one word in the public mind. In this new business model, companies seek to build one-word equity—to define the characteristic they most want instantly associated with their brand around the world, and then own it. That is one-word equity."

If any politician, let alone any company, has ever established "global ownership of one word in the public mind," it's Obama's seemingly permanent grip on "hope." Whatever your politics, you must agree that's an amazing accomplishment ....[4]"

---

[3] https://topresume.com/career-advice/7-top-job-search-statistics#:~:text=77%20
percent%20of%20recruiters%20rely%20on%20LinkedIn.%20While,you%20
are%20missing%20out%20on%20ample%20job%20opportunities.

[4] https://danpink.com/2008/06/obamas-one-word-equity/

What Word Do You Own?

Barack Obama also owned the word "change." His team expanded that into "change you can believe in." BMW owns "engineered." Apple owns "innovative" or "creative." Those would have been two words on Obama's LinkedIn profile.

Own a Sentence

In an age of communication by 280 characters, we all need to be thinking about how we communicate using fewer words. The average resume probably has a couple hundred words and it's understandable why readers spend so little time with them. If humans have only a eight-second attention span, you need to grab them quickly with a punchy message that suggests some benefit to them. Call it a profile statement, a tweet or an elevator pitch. The name doesn't matter as much as the quality and brevity of the wording.

Let me stop and tell you a story. I always ask my students, "What word do you own and how do you explain that in a sentence?" One of the students I asked told me this story:

> *I own the word 'resourceful.' One evening I was expecting a call from a recruiter and I noticed that my cell battery was dead. I had no landline and when I found my charger, it was broken. I looked around quickly as I was expecting the call in fifteen minutes. I found an old charger from an old phone version and used parts from it to cobble together a charger that would work. It did. I had the interview and I got the job. I can help you fix that which needs fixing at your company.*

A one-sentence or even a one-phrase descriptor in Hollywood is called a log line. You may remember "Diehard on a bus" (*Speed*), or "Jaws in space" (*Aliens*) or the obvious "Snakes on a plane." This is essentially what you are doing with your sentence, describing the whole story (benefit) in one sentence.

Tell Stories

You may have noticed that my student expanded his sentence into a story. Remember, storytelling is powerful. Tell stories whenever you can to be memorable. Words have power. The Christian Bible says, "In the beginning was the word." That's pretty powerful. Remember, when you tell a story, make it simple, have a twist to it or something unexpected, use concrete details, and, if possible, make it emotional. By emotional, I don't mean sad. It can be exciting, exhilarating, funny, or ... sad. My student followed this process. He didn't expect his charger to break and we didn't expect him to recreate one. The story had a small amount of tension, an obstacle he had to overcome. We cheered when he succeeded because, like him, we were anxious. A good story will do that, make you empathize with the hero, make you feel what he feels. Your customer, the employer, may want resourceful people (don't they all). When you tell a story, such as the one mentioned earlier, you show that you can deliver that quality of resourcefulness.

Craft an Elevator Pitch

It's true that you'll be in many situations where you need to introduce yourself quickly. That's where the elevator pitch comes in. What is an elevator pitch? It's not unlike the other short messages we've discussed, such as the log line. With this brief message, you follow this path: name, claim, demonstration, differentiation, and call to action. That means you say,

> Hi, I'm Joe Jobhunter. I'm an expert in machine learning and I can help you automate your processes to save you time and money. I did this for XYV Corporation and saved them 6% and I can do it for you. Unlike the others in this field, I have a degree in Artificial Intelligence from CMU. Can we discuss this in your office next Monday?

And, there you have it, an elevator pitch. Name (Joe), Claim (expert), demonstration (6 percent for XYV), differentiation (AI from CMU), and call to action (next Monday). You can write the same pitch easily following the same formula.

Back to LinkedIn

Let's put this thinking together to help you write a powerful profile statement for your LinkedIn setting.

But, first, what does my profile say? Here it is: "You can count on me to enter all relationships and engagements with great enthusiasm and optimism, keeping the audience and its needs at the center of all decisions and messaging." Any communication or marketing strategy begins with the audience. I don't want to work with anyone who doesn't understand this fact. Notice that I began, not with "I" but with a more powerful word and one that has more connection to the reader, "you."

To me, optimism and enthusiasm are key descriptors. If you dig a little deeper into my profile, you will find plenty of marketing talk and a brief bio. What might you say in your LinkedIn profile? How about, *"A young and eager graduate with industry experience ready to help the right organization achieve its goals through hard work, dedication, and self-motivation to create customers and please them."* I say this because Peter Drucker, the world-famous business guru, said that a company only has one purpose—to create (and retain) a customer.[5] Think about it. If you have no customers, you have no business. He said that this could only happen if a company practiced marketing and innovation. The only constant is change and if a company doesn't change (innovate), it will die. If it neglects its customers, it will die. Remember, Kotler said that marketing's purpose is to sense, serve, and satisfy the wants and needs of customers. That's the reason all employees are there—to sense, serve, and satisfy the wants and needs of customers. Find out quickly what your customer (hiring agent) wants and needs and show them how you can deliver it.

Write a Blog

Marketing, and other, practices also change. Anyone can follow these changes and have opinions about them. A ton of content passes through the Internet constantly. It's there for you to use, share, opine about. Blogs

---

[5] https://forbes.com/2006/06/30/jack-trout-on-marketing-cx_jt_0703drucker.html?sh=1165fbc5555c

can be Search Engine Optimization magnets, especially when you share content from other blogs and when you are addressing hot topics. You want your name to arise quickly when someone searches you on Google or another engine.

One trick you can use to build your network is to ask to interview people for your blog. Almost no one will refuse being interviewed. You make them feel like experts. This is not deceitful; it just shows an understanding of human nature.

What will I do when you interview me for your blog? After you share the content with me and allow me to edit it, I will send all of my friends and acquaintances to it. I will start to build traffic for you to help you become better known. Tell me that putting your blog on your resume won't impress someone! You can use the names of the people you've interviewed on your resume. Remember, words have power. Names have power.

To write and manage a blog takes some skills that we're not covering here. But, this communication tool can serve you well while you try to get that job. And believe me, employers want technical skills but they also want communicators.[6] As the saying goes, they'll hire you for your technical skills but fire you if you can't communicate. When you write a blog, you show some awesome communication know-how. If you don't feel comfortable writing, other platforms can help you. If you write a blog, it's best that you write often (every day) and post longer articles (3,000 words). Try to include some images and/or videos. It's a big commitment but it can pay off if you have something to say and if you invite others to contribute.

Make Facebook and Twitter Work for You

Whole books have been written about how to use these two platforms in marketing. Let's suffice it to say that a good presence on both sites can help you. I say a good presence. Lots of people are cavalier about their use of both platforms. They express too many political, social, religious, and personal matters. Remember, your social media accounts will be reviewed

---

[6] https:/indeed.com/career-advice/finding-a-job/qualities-employers-want

by recruiters. If you are too passionate about unpopular topics, you may be shunned by recruiters.

So, what do you do with Facebook and Twitter? You show your smarts. You write about topics related to the work you're seeking. A popular saying is, "Content is king!" You need to take advantage of this and create good content. You also have to follow, read, comment on, and share the content that others are posting. If you desire a great job in marketing, you need to follow Kotler, the American Marketing Association (AMA), the local chapter of the AMA, the marketing execs at Apple, Tesla, and many other innovative companies and people. Speaking of people, others know a lot more about this subject than I do. I try to keep to the fundamentals. If you write something interesting and share it with friends, you may become popular. If you write banalities, you won't.

Know the Other Social Media

Obviously you need to know how YouTube, TikTok, Instagram, Snapchat, WeChat, and other popular social media work. This is fundamental for most jobs today. Everyone is in business, whether they work for profit or not for profit. They all need customers. So, they track social media. They engage in social media. The produce content and when they do it well, they gain followers and likes and the social media gold, shares.

You are in the business of selling yourself, the Product You and the Brand You. Learn how to do it correctly on social media. Don't shoot yourself in the foot by posting inanities and inappropriate messages that will come back to haunt you.

Do Video

These days any post without a picture is not likely to be read. In fact, photos are giving way to video, as TikTok and YouTube prove. I have been using video for a few years with the #AskEd, a series of short videos (I'm talking 45–60 seconds) of information about how to communicate better.

It doesn't take much to create a good, short video—a cell phone, a light source (available light from the north is best), and a microphone that connects to your cell phone via Bluetooth. You can talk about anything. Better yet, interview people and let them talk about what excites them. This is an excellent way to get to know them and for them to get to know you. Lots of people are looking to hire talent who know how to handle social media. If you have these skills, use them.

Write a Powerful Cover Letter

You can always send someone e-mail. But, remember, all people are motivated be self-interest. Sure, we do things for others but even then we do it because it makes us feel better. If you write an e-mail, then you must appeal to the reader's self-interest, not your own. What does that mean?

When I assign my students to do this, they often write the same letter. Every letter begins with the same word. Can you guess what that word is? It is "I." Every letter says, "I am. I want. I have done this and I have done that." They are so terribly boring and lacking any creativity or understanding of the audience. How should you write one?

Remember the rules we discussed at the beginning of this book. Everyone is overloaded with messages and distracted, so you must first attract their attention. How do you do this? Use a question, quote, story, statistic, or novelty. These techniques work. Above all, use the word "you" liberally. Let me give you an example.

So, what does this letter do? It grabs attention with an interesting statistic. It differentiates the writer who speaks three languages. It connects directly to the work of the international company. It speaks to the reader using "you" liberally. It gives a concrete measureable evidence of the writer's accomplishments. It shows enthusiasm and energy and it gives a call-to-action through the questions, "Can we connect this week?"

You could begin with a quote.

You can write a letter like that, using a quote to grab the reader's attention and then using the other techniques I discussed in the previous letter, call-to-action, the word "you," example of accomplishments. If those approaches don't work for you, try this one. It will definitely grab attention, trust me!

Imagine someone writing for a job and beginning their letter by saying, "I don't want a job." That creates cognitive dissonance and it will grab

---

A Sample Cover Letter

Dear Friend:

Statistics show that 5127 students will graduate from marketing programs in US colleges this year. What the statistics don't show is that only one of them will speak English, French, Spanish and a few words of German. That person is me.

Because your company does work internationally, you will benefit from staff who speak other languages and who have visited other countries. Of course, you need staff who know the fundamentals of marketing and who have practiced those fundamentals in internships. You will find, herein, the resume of one such person.

You will find a person who has worked successfully in teams on projects that required measurable results, such as a product introduction for ABZ that resulted in a 14% increase in sales over previous product launches. You will find a self-motivated person whose values and ethics match those of your company, someone who has given time over three summers to feed the homeless of Pittsburgh.

The marketing specialist position that you have available matches this person perfectly. He is ready at a moment's notice to connect with you to show you, face-to-face, his energy, enthusiasm and desire. Can we connect this week? I await your reply.

---

attention. It's risky, of course, but nothing great was ever gained without some risk.

Here's one last example, this one using a story.

So, in this latter example, we have, of course, begun with a story. Stories have great power. We tell stories every day, not fictions, but narratives that help us understand how to live together, how to avoid pitfalls, how to live our lives. Don't overlook the power of stories to make yourself persuasive.

The last one is questioning. You can begin an e-mail by asking a question. Questions invite participation. When I ask you a question, you feel the need to answer, to participate with me. So, if I wrote to your company and said, in the first sentence, "What kind of employee does ABZ want

---

Another Sample Cover Letter

Dear Friend:

Philip Kotler, one of the world's experts in marketing, said, "A good company offers excellent products and services. A great company also offers excellent products and services but also strives to make the world a better place."

Your company has shown this philosophy through its interaction and support of International Women's Day this year. Your campaign to "Raise Your Hands" was a success, as reported in the national media. It was truly an effort to make the world a better place.

You must be very proud of the work that ABZ does to bring, not just great products to the world, but greater understanding and collaboration. This quality makes many of us new graduates want to work for ABZ. And, you want people who reflect your values and commitments.

Of course, you need staff who know the fundamentals of marketing and who have practiced those fundamentals in internships. You will find, herein, the resume of one such person.

You will find a person who has worked successfully in teams on projects that required measurable results, such as a product introduction for ABZ that resulted in a 14% increase in sales over previous product launches. You will find a self-motivated person whose values and ethics match those of your company, someone who has given time over three summers to feed the homeless of Pittsburgh.

The marketing specialist position that you have available matches this person perfectly. He is ready at a moment's notice to connect with you to show you, face-to-face, his energy, enthusiasm and desire. Can we connect this week? I await your reply.

---

to hire?" the reader will know the answer and want to see if you do. That's when you say, in the next sentence, "ABZ wants self-motivated, experienced, mature, ethical team players who bring energy and enthusiasm to the job every day."

A Third Sample Cover Letter

Dear Friend,

I don't want a JOB at ABZ.

So, why am I writing to you? I want a CAREER at ABZ. I want to go to work every day for the next 20 years being proud of the place where I work, a company that has values, such as teamwork, innovation and collaboration.

ABZ has these values and more. You have proven through your recent product launch of SlipperySoap that you understand the needs and motivations of parents who have young children. Your creative was exceptional, your distribution was timely and the price fit the needs of young parents. But, more than that, your very public support of International Woman's Day told the world where ABZ stands on the issues that divide us.

This quality makes many of us new graduates want to work for ABZ. And, you want people who reflect your values and commitments.

Of course, you need staff who know the fundamentals of marketing and who have practiced those fundamentals in internships. You will find, herein, the resume of one such person.

You will find a person who has worked successfully in teams on projects that required measurable results, such as a product introduction for XYZ that resulted in a 14% increase in sales over previous product launches. You will find a self-motivated person whose values and ethics match those of your company, someone who has given time over three summers to feed the homeless of Pittsburgh.

The marketing specialist position that you have available matches this person perfectly. He is ready at a moment's notice to connect with you to show you, face-to-face, his energy, enthusiasm and desire. Can we connect this week? I await your reply.

A Fourth Sample Cover Letter

Dear Friend:

When I visited India last year, I saw a young woman trying to feed her baby while she worked at a plant where dyes were used to make clothing. Working in harsh chemicals, both she and her little girl were covered in blue from the dyes being used. When I asked about the hours she worked and the salary she was paid, I was told that she worked ten hours each day and made the equivalent of $25. That's when I was so proud of companies like yours who have taken a stand on women's issues by sponsoring International Woman's Day.

You have proven that you care about people. You have also proven your marketing talent through your recent product launch of SlipperySoap. You clearly understand the needs and motivations of parents who have young children. Your creative was exceptional, your distribution was timely, and the price fit the needs of young parents. These qualities makes many of us new graduates want to work for ABZ. And, you want people who reflect your values and commitments.

Of course, you need staff who know the fundamentals of marketing and who have practiced those fundamentals in internships. You will find, herein, the resume of one such person.

You will find a person who has worked successfully in teams on projects that required measurable results, such as a product introduction for ABZ that resulted in a 14% increase in sales over previous product launches. You will find a self-motivated person whose values and ethics match those of your company, someone who has given time over three summers to feed the homeless of Pittsburgh.

The marketing specialist position that you have available matches this person perfectly. He is ready at a moment's notice to connect with you to show you, face-to-face, his energy, enthusiasm and desire. Can we connect this week? I await your reply.

Key Concepts

Most people get jobs through networking.

You can build a network easily.

You can become known through LinkedIn and other promotional activity.

To be liked, be interested, not interesting. Listen more than you talk.

Prepare an elevator pitch.

Own a word.

Turn your word into a sentence and turn that into a story.

Make social media work for you. Start a blog. Tweet. Post. Be visible.

When you write to someone, focus on them, not on yourself. Avoid the "I" word.

Answer These Questions

What word do I own?_____

How is that word part of my promise (pitch, slogan, or sentence)?

_____

What story can I tell that will exemplify that word (quality)?

_____

What is my elevator pitch?

_____

CHAPTER 9

The Many Ways of Finding Job Opportunities

If you can't volunteer, take an internship, or spend time trying to ingratiate yourself with potential employers, use the paths of least resistance. But, remember, this whole book is based on a few important principles—you are marketing yourself, marketing is objectivity, planning brings power, marketing techniques apply to getting a job, everyone is self-interested. Add to those another principle—there are the typical ways of finding a job and the successful candidate tries them all.

Job Sites

I have found over the years that a person can land a job in many different ways and it is best to try each way. Networking is the most popular way today. The only trouble with networking is that students and others looking for work have no concept of what to do while networking. They are not told what you have already been told in this book and what you will also hear.

Search firms are a popular way to find a job. Companies like Robert Half, a global human resource consulting firm, are not for everyone, however. Some of these firms ask you to pay fees. If you are in a position to do that, you might want to look at them.

The Internet is the means for finding a good job, especially tech jobs at young companies. Most people who read the postings to find a job only look at very specific ads like "writer," "PR specialist," "customer service rep." My advice is to look at every job listed. I say this because often employers are not sure what to call the position they are advertising to fill. They may think it's a "clerical" function when in fact it's a "PR" function.

How often have you seen it the other way around? The job says "Great opportunity for an entry-level PR person" and the job turns out to be a secretarial one.

I say, "Apply to everything." Why do I say that? For several reasons. Applying for jobs is a tedious, depressing, direct mail promotional activity. Why not have some fun with it? Apply for presidencies. Why not? Why tell yourself, "No?" Let them tell you, "No." Apply for clerical positions. This is your chance to tell someone else, "No." Really! Remember our old friend Jimmy Carter. Here's a guy who was a peanut farmer, for God's sake, and said to himself, "I think I'll become President of the United States." Very few corporate presidents were born into the job. I say you should e-mail 100 messages, expecting to receive 10 responses and 1 job. It's direct mail at work.

Available Opportunities

Don't dismiss any job opportunity because it isn't exactly what you want at the moment or the title doesn't happen to state exactly what work you're available for. Again, often the people who write Wanted Ads, or just the job titles, don't know exactly what to call what it is they're after. This is especially true of smaller companies and often they're the best ones to work for. Don't you wish you would have applied to a small company called Microsoft a few years ago and bought a couple hundred shares for next to nothing. Or a small company called Dell, or AOL, or eBay. Give every job opening its due. You may be one of the next millionaires.

Other Angles

Get your resume into the hands of everyone you can think of—relatives, friends, friends' parents, neighbors, casual acquaintances, search firms, web sites, professors, adjuncts—anyone who may hear about a job opening and be able to help you. People want to help you, out of selfishness. They want to feel like good guys, heroines, mentors, Godfathers, big shots. They want to say, after you've become a millionaire, "I helped that kid when she was a nobody."

The "Insurance Executive" Story

I once read a story about a man who had been appointed as CEO of a large insurance company. The story said that he had been raised in a small town, was the first person in his family to attend college, had become a school teacher, a wrestling coach, had left teaching and entered the wonderful world of marketing. Because I was interested in a career move, I wrote to him and told him about a man who was raised in a small town (me), was the first person in the family to attend college (me), became a teacher (you guessed it, me), a wrestling coach, and a marketer. I told him I was interested in a career move. The CEO wrote back to me in a week and joked about our similar backgrounds. He told me there were no immediate openings for someone of my talents but forwarded my resume to his Vice President of Human Resources.

I thought I'd never hear from them again, but low and behold the VP called me within a week and set up an interview. He acknowledged there were no immediate openings but we had a good, in-depth interview and I increased my network by one. Who knows, I may never hear from them, but then again … .

Key Concepts

There are standard ways to find a job and nonstandard ways as well. Look for all of them.

Apply to different types of jobs. Sometimes the only way in is to get in.

If you had applied to Apple many years ago and been given stock, you'd be happy today.

CHAPTER 10

Job Search Marketing Stories From the Trenches

The "Late Tom" Story

I'll never forget Tom. I was interviewing for an assistant director of the department. He called my secretary to say he'd be 15 minutes late for the two o'clock interview. I was OK with that. He had the good sense to call. When two-fifteen o'clock rolled around, Tom was nowhere to be seen. At two-thirty, he was still among the absent. Now, I have a reputation for being chronically early. I can't stand to be late. My wife, God bless her, is the same way. Anyway, while I waited for Tom, I talked to myself. "Be calm, Ed. Give him a chance to explain himself. It could be something awful." Over the years, I have learned that if someone were late it might mean a tragedy in their family. So, I chewed my pencil and tapped my foot while waiting for Tom.

At 3:00 p.m. Tom showed up at my door. My first impression was of a disheveled young man, attaché case in hand, rumpled trench coat covering a brown sports coat. "Sorry I'm late," Tom said and I invited him into the office.

I decided I wasn't going to say anything until Tom explained himself. He sat in the chair in front of my desk, squirmed out of his trench coat, tightened the knot in his tie, rotated his head as if to work the kinks out of his neck, tugged at his jacket, cleared his throat, and looked at me.

We looked at each other for an uncomfortably long time until I finally said, "Where were you?"

"I'm doing some consulting work and I was with a client," he responded. "I didn't want to leave until we were finished."

"Don't you think it's important to be on time?" I asked.

"I called to say I'd be late," he replied.

I was struggling to remain composed. "Well, then, don't you think it's important to schedule your time better?"

"I suppose so," he said, "but sometimes the best schedule breaks down."

What's the message here? There are two messages. One, don't be late for an interview, period. If you must, leave an hour ahead of schedule. Be at the company with plenty of time to look around and gather the kinds of information I mentioned before. The second message is, I remember Tom. I remember him because he was different; he was late. I didn't hire Tom but it was not because he was late. He didn't have the requisite skills, especially as compared to other recruits. But, it also didn't help that he was late. It gave a bad first impression.

The "Spiked Hair" Story

Another interview I remember involved a college senior. She stunned me with her looks. Her hair was green and spiked straight up in the air. I worked for a Catholic hospital that prided itself in cultural diversity; we were all tuned into "difference." And, we should have been. This young lady was bright, energetic, and fun. I would have hired her if it were not that we had a stronger all-around candidate. I liked her confidence, her poise, her comfort with herself. Those qualities are missing in many employees, unfortunately. I learned from that young woman not to judge a book by its cover. Thank you, Punk, wherever you are.

The "Sheri" Story

Once I interviewed several people for a very important position, News Media Coordinator. It was very important to me because I had spent a few years building a positive relationship with the area media and needed to turn the responsibility over to someone else. I interviewed 10 candidates and narrowed the list to two young women, both energetic, eager, bright, and well educated. One of them had direct experience, the other, Sheri, whom I knew from her student days at a college where I worked, had little direct experience. Sheri made it to the finals because she was a woman of integrity and focus. I knew she could do the job, but the other woman was compelling, especially in her two years of direct experience in a competitor organization. The choice was difficult. I labored over the decision until one evening at the close of work Sheri stopped by my office to deliver what I believed was a sappy letter thanking me for the interview. Instead, what Sheri delivered was a news release she had created announcing that she had been chosen for the position of News Media Coordinator. My decision was made. I appointed Sheri to the job and she was outstanding until she left to join one of the major PR firms in town. She now has her own business.

Every interview is a little different, but some things remains the same: you must differentiate yourself; you must give the hiring agent a reason to remember you; you must be authentic; you must be interested in the person interviewing you, not interesting; you must understand the wants and needs of the customer (the employer).

My "Charlotte" Story

I was once contacted by a search firm regarding an executive position in South Carolina. I was stoked. The telephone interview with the search firm went well. Their review of my credentials went well. They scheduled an interview with me at the local airport. That went extremely well, too. I was on a roll. They scheduled me for a meeting at the Charlotte, North Carolina airport where other candidates were joining me to be separately interviewed. I was psyched. I was in top form. I kicked butt at the interview, even though the executive who interviewed me seemed perfunctory. I felt there was no way they could deny me. My education is good, my experience is impeccable, everything was in order. I flew back home thinking of the resignation letter I'd have to write, friends I'd have to tell, and moving arrangements I'd have to make. I was sad to think of leaving friends but happy to be moving up in the ranks and making the big bucks. You can imagine my disappointment when the search firm called to say the company had offered the position to someone else.

I was baffled. As I questioned the firm's rep I discovered the guy in Charlotte had offered the position to someone he knew from his previous place of employment. No wonder he was perfunctory, he had someone else in mind the whole time. He was going through the motions with me and never intended to offer the job to anyone but his buddy from home.

What's the take-away? Sometimes the cards are stacked against you. You may have done an excellent job in the interview and had all the requirements. Sometimes to satisfy the law, employers go through the motions when they already have a candidate in hand.

The "Karl" Story

I'll never forget a guy I hired who talked a good game but turned out to be a bad hire. Let's call him "Karl."

Karl was in one of my graduate classes. He was a salesman who was finishing a degree in PR so that he could change careers. In class he was attentive, curious, participative, and bright. He had good writing skills and seemed to have a natural talent for knowing what makes a good news story. Because of his sales background, he understood goal setting. He was interested in current events, including sports and politics. He was a good conversationalist. He seemed like the perfect candidate for a PR job. I told him I would help lead him to a network of PR people and that if he ever needed a reference for a PR job or if I ever had an opening I would consider him.

As luck (his, not mine) would have it, within a year of our class, we had an opening in our department and after a thorough interviewing process, we hired Karl. He interviewed well and impressed everyone on the staff. He settled into the job (cemented himself to the seat of his chair is more like it). In true Jekyll-Hide fashion, Karl became another person. He held court in his office almost all day giving forth his opinions about everything from John Kennedy to the Pittsburgh Penguins. He was all talk and no walk. I was extremely disappointed. In a few months, he returned to his job in sales where I assume he did well.

CHAPTER 11

The Sales Pitch

The Interview is your sales pitch.

OK, so you get to the interview. How should you act? You should model the Four "E's"—enthusiasm, energy, education, and engagement.

Use the Four E's: Enthusiasm, Energy, Education, and Engagement

Enthusiasm and Energy

You should sit facing your interviewer and maintaining eye contact. You should make me, the interviewer, feel like the most important person in the world. Remember, the interview is NOT about you. It's about the interviewer and her needs. As far as I'm concerned, you're there to validate the greatness and wisdom of the person interviewing you, me!

Whoever's interviewing you knows he's not buying a finished product. I don't care who it is, in what position, there's a learning curve even for vice presidents. It will take you a while to get "up to speed," even if you "hit the ground running." I look for someone who is enthusiastic and energetic, someone who is eager to learn. I can find that, to some extent, in their resume and cover letter (special accomplishments) but nothing is as revealing as the face-to-face interview.

So, what does an enthused and energetic person look like. First, it's someone who had a good night's sleep the night before, someone who is fresh and bright, whose clothes are clean and pressed. Aha, you're saying, what about the punk with the spiked hair? The answer is that she was clean, bright, and wired with energy. She was enthusiastic. (Enthusiasm comes from the Greek roots "en theos" or "with God, that is, "spirited." Be spirited!) But, she didn't have the hard skills or experience we needed. She was, however, a great person and I was happy to help her by connecting her to people I knew who might have been looking for a good designer.

Your attentiveness and posture speak to your energy and enthusiasm. You should sit straight and lean slightly toward me and ask appropriate questions. Some of these questions are:

Is there a job description for this position? May I see a copy? (Warning! Don't ever accept a job without a position description. Volunteer to write it yourself, if necessary.)

Does each employee have a performance plan? (Warning! If not, offer to write a plan for your position with six- and twelve-month objectives. It's best to negotiate exactly what your performance will be measured on in specific, measurable terms.)

What, if I may ask, is the budget for the department, or this position? (Ask politely because it may be guarded information.)

What is your management style?

How would your other employees describe you?

What is your decision-making process for this position?

How would you describe the corporate culture?

Who is the company's competition?

What is the management like (men? women?)

Don't rattle off these questions as if you were the prosecuting attorney. Ask them at the appropriate times with genuine interest. It gives you a chance to impress the interviewer and for her to show off a little. Nothing is quite as boring or difficult as carrying on a conversation with someone who gives one-word answers and doesn't engage in the conversation by asking questions and commenting on the statements made by the other person. If you're at a networking event, a party, or an interview, it's the same. You need to be a good conversationalist.

Are there people who will interview you and talk endlessly? Yes. Are there people who will ask you one question and expect you to carry the conversation? Yes. Are there interviewers who are just going through the motions? Yes. Some of them made up their minds long before you arrived. What do you do in this case? Chalk it up to experience. Some days you eat the bear and some days the bear eats you. Sometimes there's no rhyme or reason to getting a job. I have gotten jobs because of political connections, wanted ads, search firms, friends, being in the right place at the right time. The best thing to do, again, is use all your resources. Throw a lot of lines in the river and wait for a bite.

Do the best you can in an interview even if you think it is going poorly. An associate of mine went on an interview for a position in a bank. The Human Resources (HR) representative greeted her and placed her in a room with a long table and she seated herself at the end of the table. The interviewer entered and sat at the direct other end of the table. During the entire interview, he did not make eye contact once, although she tried to make eye contact. He stared at the table or the wall. Starting the interview, he fired one question after another at her offering no feedback or follow-up questions to any of her answers. Yet, she continued to answer with enthusiasm and energy. Walking out of the interview, she definitely thought she did not get the position. The next day, the HR representative called and offered her the job. Moral of the story: no matter how poorly you think an interview is going stay in there and give it your best shot.

Education and Engagement

You definitely need to be educated about the business of the person interviewing you, but don't pretend you know more than you do. In fact, you're better deferring to the knowledge of the interviewer. Remember, we're trying to make her the hero, the omniscient, omnipotent one. For instance, if you're applying for a job in health care, you should know something about managed care since it has revolutionized health care delivery at the end of the 20th century. This is not to say that you should be articulate about health maintenance organization, preferred provide organization, and the other alphabet of modern health care. It just means you enough to engage in a brief conversation.

Spending an hour in a room with a stranger, especially one who is inanimate, is deadly. You need to be engaging. That means you need to ask intelligent questions and make intelligent, interesting statements. If necessary, you need to rehearse for your interview. Ask a friend to sit with you and conduct a "mock interview." You need to be prepared. You only get one chance. If you're engaging, you may get a second interview. All of us busy executives want an excuse to hire someone as quickly as possible, but the stakes are so great we typically interview candidates several times and have our staff interview them, as well.

Sometimes there are tests involved. Basic skill tests like writing or addition are often given. I don't test candidates. For instance, I do not apply writing tests to potential writers nor do I ask them to bring a stack of writing samples. I do, however, ask them what they believe to be a good piece of writing. Typically, they stumble on this. If they answer "Les Miserables," "Moby Dick," or any modern piece of writing by contemporary masters like Raymond Carver, I'll understand they know what they're talking about. If they spent four years in college and two in graduate school, they should have some idea about how to write (although I don't assume they are good writers).

The Last Question

You should ask your interviewer a last question and that is—"How did I do?" It's important for you to receive feedback. If she is honest, the interviewer will be surprised but tell you what she perceives were your strengths and weaknesses. The others will be surprised and disarmed and stutter and stammer. They'll avoid answering you because they don't want to compromise themselves. They'll say nothing and the next likely communication you'll receive is a form letter telling you how wonderful you are but how they "found a candidate whose credentials and experience more closely matched the requirements for the position …." This has happened to me and I've thought I'm better off not having worked for those people.

Keep track of your interviews and learn from them. Evaluate your performance think about what went well and what didn't. Consider the experiences as opportunities to grow.

Key Concepts

The interview is your "sales pitch." Prepare for it. Focus on their needs.

Show enthusiasm and energy in your interview. Use your voice and body language effectively.

Know about the business of the company where you're interviewing. Prepare in advance. Educate yourself.

Engage the interviewer. Ask questions.

My Interview Log

Company	Interviewer	Positives	Negatives	Opportunity

CHAPTER 12

The Follow Up

Marketing is often described as "sales." Like advertising and promotion, sales is a visible part of marketing and an important part. If you call on a potential client to pitch your product and that person refuses, you don't throw up your hands and walk away mad. You want to build a relationship so that when that person has a need for your product he will think of you.

Follow up is, therefore, an important part of marketing. It's also an important part of a job search. If possible, you want to continue some kind of relationship with the people who interview you. If possible, you want to do something for them.

After the Interview

The interview has ended and you, like every other candidate, have been told by most to send a follow-up message. I always received versions of the same boring "thank you" letters after I interviewed people. It's not that I don't appreciate their gratitude, but every letter sounded the same. They appreciated the opportunity to meet with me and my staff (whom they sometimes name so as to show how much they paid attention) and to learn more about the corporation. They know they will be an asset to the organization and look forward to hearing from me in the very near future. The real daring ones say they'll call.

The trouble is these letters all say the same thing. And, I know why they do it. Some told them it's what they should do and gave them a form letter. Remember that a format of anything (resume, cover letter) does not differentiate you or demonstrate any knowledge of marketing, understanding each audience.

I'd really like to get a letter from someone who knows the interview process is cumbersome and unnatural (it really is; it's an unnatural process), who knows it's damn near impossible to learn enough about a prospective employee after an hour, who knows taking a job is like taking a spouse. So, write me a letter or e-mail, by all means, but make it interesting. Anything you write competes with anything that's written. It's competing for limited attention span. It needs to do what every successful message must do: grab my attention, interest me, and motivate me in some way. A form letter will not do that.

So, it's time for your test. What ways did we discuss that grab attention? Right, questions, quotes, stories, statistics, novelty. What is the most powerful word in marketing? No, it's not "free," although that's very powerful. It's "you." Above all that, you must put yourself in my shoes, the guy who's receiving a boatload of thank you messages.

What might your message look like?

Sample Thank You Message

Dear Person Who Holds My Future in Your Hands (real name)

You must be very happy that you're getting closer to choosing the best candidate for the AI position. I can imagine how tiring it must be to sit through so many interviews after reviewing so many resumes. Knowing how hard that must be, I thank you for taking time with me to discuss the AI position at XYV Corporation.

Your suggestion that AI will be a major force in the world in the 21st Century makes sense to me; I'm happy that I chose that field and that I studied at Carnegie Mellon, one of the premier schools in AI.

Much is being written about AI and I thought the article in the link below would interest you. It talks about AI in manufacturing. If you haven't already read it, I promise you will enjoy it. (LINK)

As your deadline rolls around for filling the AI position, I thank you, once again, for allowing me to share my credentials and enumerate the many ways I know I can help XYZ Corporation.

Best wishes,
Jenny Jobseeker

If you examine the sample letter, you will see that I begin with "you" and try to make the letter, not about me, but about her. In the second paragraph, I acknowledge something that she said during the interview. It makes her see that I was listening and that I believe she has important things to say. Again, this is about her, not me. In the rest of the message, I remind her that I have good credentials in AI. Then, I do something powerful; I give her something, a link to an interesting article, one that I know she will enjoy. Even if she's already read it, she will be impressed that I have shared it. This is a powerful tool of influence called, "reciprocity." If we are given something, we feel compelled to return the favor, to give something in return. Does that mean she will give you the job? No. But, it definitely works in your favor.

Reciprocity is just one process that helps us influence someone. The others include social proof, commitment/consistency, liking, authority, and scarcity. You can use these in many relationships as long as you use them ethically and correctly. They have great power. When you give someone something (reciprocity), as we said, they feel a powerful compulsion to give you something in return. When you show social proof, such as reference letters, you show that others have a high regard for you. This suggests that the person viewing the letter should also have high regard for you. If you can lead a person to make a small commitment, that person will continue to make similar commitments because of consistency. For instance, if you persuade someone to let you volunteer for a day or a week, that person will likely let you continue for more days and weeks, and perhaps hire you. If you want people to like you, then be like them. Dress like them, talk like them, walk like them. Imitation is the sincerest form of flattery. You can persuade with authority by bringing all your credentials to the table, all of them, even certificates, even an Eagle Scout achievement. Lastly, you can influence by being scarce. If you have another job offer, or if you have second interviews pending, or other job opportunities, you may want to reveal them. You're telling a potential hiring agent that you may become scarce if they don't act soon by hiring you. This last one can backfire if not handled well. And, Robert Cialdini, who wrote the book, *Influence*, admonishes us to use these powerful persuaders ethically.

Social Media Connections

Consider asking the person who interviewed you for a LinkedIn connection. You can do this after the interview, in the message that you send as a follow up, or simply by using the LinkedIn connection in their app. I feel good when people want to connect with me and I like to build my connections, especially with younger people. (If you're reading this, please reach out to me. I will accept your request.) I also stay active on Facebook and love to make connections there. I have a presence on WeChat, Weibo, and other social media. I'm a sociable guy!

Telephone Calls, Don't Make Them

The last things you want a recruiter to think about you is that you are desperate. If you call to ask about the status of the selection process, you look desperate. Also, if you put your faith and efforts into just one potential job, you are making a mistake. Apply for positions at several companies. It's nice to know that you have opportunities and that you will have a choice in the matter. Wouldn't it be nice if they fought over you?!

Key Concepts

Products (you) are more memorable if you are differentiated.

Everyone sends a thank you message after an interview but few are different or interesting.

"YOU" is a powerful word because we are all motivated by self-interest.

In marketing, we concentrate on the customer (audience), its needs, and wants.

Everyone is overwhelmed with messages; make yours count.

CHAPTER 13

How Do Buyers Make Decisions?

Are They Conscious?

Science tells us that we live our lives mostly unconsciously. We fly on automatic pilot. Scholars tell us we think with two systems, System 1 and System 2. System 1 is also called "thinking fast" and System 2 is called "thinking slow." Nobel Prize laureate, Daniel Kahneman, popularized these terms.[1] When we "think" in System 1, we are likely to make some mistakes because we have unconscious biases. We are also told that we buy emotionally and then justify rationally. This has huge implications in our lives. We think we are thinking but we are making decisions before we think about them, that is, cogitate. The same thing happens during interviews and salary negotiations.

Anchoring

Earlier in this book, we talked about "framing" and "priming" and "confirmation bias." Let's talk a little about anchoring. Your mind can be biased when an anchor is presented. Let's say you are negotiating a job salary. You'd like to receive $100,000 per year. Should you say that? It depends. When you say that number, you have anchored the mind of the other person on that number. Chances are, they will then make an offer below $100,000. Chances also exit that they were ready to set their anchor at $125,000. Anchors are powerful and we are mostly unconscious of them. If a real estate agent takes you to look at a $1,000,000 home, you are

---

[1] https://en.wikipedia.org/wiki/Thinking,_Fast_and_Slow

likely to feel very good about the $750,000 home he next shows you. You are also not likely to know that you have been affected by an anchor.

Back to the salary offer. I have taught students that when asked for their salary needs, they should say, "I'd like a million dollars." It sounds like a joke and lightens the discussion but it also sets an anchor. You unconsciously begin to negotiate down from there!

Maslow's Hierarch of Needs

We base marketing on a thorough understanding of the customer. That means we must understand them as humans, just like us, who have, as we said, many wants and needs. Years ago, Abraham Maslow, an American psychologist, devised what he believed to be the common needs of all people. These needs were placed into levels that represent: physiological needs, as well as the needs for safety, love, esteem, self-actualization, and transcendence.

What does this have to do with getting a job? It means that the recruiters want to feel safe around you, they want to trust you, they want to be respected, they want to feel esteemed. Look, we all want these! It's not a bad thing, then, to make others (recruiters) feel important. I'm not talking about flattery. I mean simple, human kindness, the kindness to compliment the recruiters, to make them feel esteemed, to somehow show them that you can be trusted.

One of our most primal instincts is fear. We even have a special set of neurons in our brains called the amygdalae to help us deal with fear. If we didn't our species may not have survived. We use smiles to show our warmth and our intention. Smiles, genuine smiles, show that we mean no harm.

Warmth and Competence

In a Harvard Business Review article, author Heidi Grant, said this, "… the most important thing to get across in an interview is not that you are smart and motivated—it's that you are trustworthy … Trustworthiness is the fundamental trait that people—not just interviewers—automatically and unconsciously look for in others. It will make or break you."

Ms. Grant continues her discussion by focusing on the two most important qualities, warmth and competence. She says, "… as countless *studies by Harvard's Amy Cuddy* and others have shown, there are two qualities you need to possess to be seen as trustworthy: *warmth* and *competence*. Warmth signals that you have good intentions toward the perceiver, and competence signals that you can act on those good intentions. A warm and competent interviewee is a valuable potential ally. But a competent interviewee who doesn't project warmth is a potentially formidable foe—the kind of person who may not be a team player, and who may cause trouble for you down the road.²"

Are you projecting warmth? Are you allowing the other person to feel safe? Is the interviewer consciously evaluating your warmth? It's more likely that these considerations are going on unconsciously, or as they say, under the radar.

Use a Clipboard

Did you know that in a research experiment, job candidates who handed their resumes to recruiters on a heavy clipboard were perceived to be "weightier," more impressive? Did you know that getting your interviewer to nod his head up and down will make him more agreeable³? Do you think that the person who gets the clipboard and the person who nods his head know what is happening to them? I seriously doubt it. Research has shown that even when you tell people that you are priming them, they refuse to believe that they made their decisions by being primed.

Do You Know What Your Body Language Is Saying?

Marketers, especially in the sales department, learn quickly to read the body language of their customers. They look at everything, from the eyebrows to the feet. Many good books have been written about body language, so if you want to sell yourself you should pick one up soon. (I recommend the books by Allan and Barbara Pease. You can find information about

---

² https://hbr.org/2015/05/how-to-show-trustworthiness-in-a-job-interview
³ https://inc.com/11-body-language-essentials-for-your-next-negotiation.html

their books here: https://www.peaseinternational.com/body-language/) One item is worth mentioning in regard to body language. When you are excited, the pupils of your eyes dilate. Chinese gem traders watched the eyes of buyers and knew when a buyer was interested. They used that information to pursue the sale. Watch your interviewer closely (but don't stare). Are his pupils dilating at any point in your conversation? Have you excited him by anything you've said. Or, did his eyes dilate because of fear. This also happens. In any event, body language reveals clues without our conscious knowledge. If his arms are crossed, he may be cold or he may be judgmental. Look at all the signals in combination.

Mirroring

It's always a good idea to mirror the person across from you, for instance. Don't ape them or they will dislike you, but subtly mirror their crossed arms or legs, their hand gestures, their words. We like people who are like us as Robert Cialdini's book tell us.

Cultural Considerations

Cultures differ, particularly eastern and western cultures. You need to understand the culture of your customer, the hiring agent. Eastern and western cultures differ along a number of dimensions. These include: the ways they communicate, how they reason, how they view hierarchy, how they develop and maintain relationships, how they deal with confrontation, and how they treat time. If you want to read an excellent book on these cultural matters, buy a copy of *The Culture Map* by Erin Meyer at her website: https://erinmeyer.com/books/the-culture-map/.

In a nutshell, people communicate with either a lot of context or little context. Americans do the latter. Americans also reason deductively, providing the bottom line up front. People from Asia typically give lots of evidence before they give any conclusions. They also avoid confrontation, unlike westerners. Americans say that "all people are created equal" and try to manage others in that way; whereas people in Japan, for instance, adhere to a rigid hierarchy. And, people from Asia have a looser sense of time than the clock-obsessed Americans.

I have visited India many times and I recounted one such visit earlier, a visit where I was the beneficiary of respect for the aged. What I didn't say about those visits with very high profile executives was that they almost never began on schedule. They had a different sense of time than we did. In fact, we were always early! We suffered a little bit of frustration until the time thing occurred to us.

You Can Never Ever Know Enough

As I've said numerous times, when you are marketing, you must think from the outside in, not the inside out. Know you customer. If you want to be successful, forget your wants and desires, focus on the customers' wants and needs. Socrates said, "To know thyself is the beginning of wisdom,[4]" and the Delphic Oracles inscribed "Know thyself" on the Temple of Apollo. It's good advice but not the greatest advice for marketing. For us it's "Know the other."

Key Concepts

Neuroscientists say that we live most of our lives nonconsciously.
We make decisions that we're not aware.
When you know about people's cultures, it helps you understand them.

---

[4] https://en.wikipedia.org/wiki/Know_thyself

CHAPTER 14

Always Use a Marketing Approach

A marketing approach tells us everything we need to know about interacting with others, whether in a job interview, a dating situation, a family discussion, or any other circumstance where we are trying to influence someone else.

Marketing means objectivity. I can't stress it enough. Objectivity means you focus on the wants and needs of the other person, not yourself, even when that other person doesn't understand his own wants and needs. You have to step out of yourself, your own ego, your own agenda, and your own self-interest long enough to see things through the eyes of the other.

When you can do this, you will write persuasive messages, ones that attract attention and create interest, ones that are read and acted upon, such as your cover letter, e-mail, resume, person-to-person communications, and interviews. You will talk less about yourself. You will ask more questions. You will listen more.

Does this guarantee you a job? No. That guarantee doesn't exist, unless your family owns the business. Too many variables exist, just as they do with any company trying to influence customers. Then there's the competition. We could spend a lot of time discussing the strategies that marketers use to deal with their competition. In any event, a marketing approach will take you closer to your goal, especially if the competition doesn't use the approach.

Remember the 4 P's

For over 50 years, the 4 P's have stood the test of time with marketers. Today, many may be using different formulas, but they all mean the same, basically, whether it's the 4 C's or some other letter of the alphabet. Remember these.

Product—You are the product/service being offered to fulfill some need of the customer, the hiring agent.

Price—You have a salary need and the hiring agent typically has a salary scale. Your ability to negotiate fills in the difference.

Place—You will be asked to work in a certain place. This may be a deal maker or deal breaker.

Promotion—This is the most visible aspect of marketing, the one that everyone defines as marketing. It is critically important because it identifies you though first impression (packaging) and messaging.

The Other P's

Positioning—This is a critical part of the marketing mix. It differentiates you when you do it well. You leave the ranks of commodities and become a one-of-a-kind product.

Politics—Sometimes it's not what you know but who you know. Don't ever discount the power of this "P" because the majority of jobs are filled through networks. Get connected to as many people as you can through social media and associations. Extend your network. Create plans and measure your effectiveness.

Write Interesting Materials

These are reading materials and, although they shouldn't read like romance novels, they are, in effect, competing with every other piece of printed material an employer has to read. Think about the poor recruiter who is reading some version of the same cover letter and resume all day. Do her a favor: write something interesting. Take a Chance. Be Human. Separate yourself from the herd. Have no fear. Be special.

Accentuate the Positive

Provide specific, measurable information about your special accomplishments, regardless of what they were, the more differentiated, the better.

Suppose you started a worm farm when you were a kid and sold worms to fishermen. How many people do you think have done that for a living? Very few. It's interesting and says volumes about your self-motivation. It will be remembered. Trust me. Don't dismiss anything you've done over the years. It's not what you did but how you tell about it. Make it interesting.

Remember: It's a Dynamic

You must have the attitude that you are selecting the employer as much as they are selecting you. I'm not talking about an arrogant attitude, just one of quiet confidence. As someone who has hired people, I want someone I don't have to follow around and jump start every other day. Too often, this is the kind of employee we end up with, too passive. Do your job but bring added value. When salespeople sell, they talk about this added value, especially with commodities. In many ways, you are a commodity; you are one of a handful of candidates who seem to fit the job description. Funny how employers bring together a bunch of people who all look the same on paper. What do they expect to get from that?

Have a Good Plan

A good plan helps you get a job, keep a job, and succeed. Very few people bother to think things through. If you appreciate and understand your company's mission, values, and strategic objective and then fit yourself to them, you will be poised for success. Remember, there is more work in every organization than there are people willing to perform that work.

Planning gives you a technique for accomplishing the corporation's objectives. It helps you determine objectives, budgets, return on investment. It gives you authority over people, sometimes even the CEO. Planning gives you power. Take that power. Use it. Use it to accomplish good ends and to advance yourself in the meantime.

How Does a Person Really Get a Job?

In my life I have obtained jobs in many different ways: wanted ads, friends, politicians, relatives, search firms. I actually got two of the best jobs I ever had by seeing them advertised in the newspaper (that was a long time ago). You never know what's going to work and for that reason you should try everything.

The Process Is Way Too Involved

Anytime someone good leaves a job in a large company, it's traumatic. We know that, at best, we'll have the job filled within eight weeks. That's at best. Why so long? As I said earlier, we have to prepare the position requisition and have it approved. That means, in effect, we have to prove all over again that we really need the position. The boss has to review it, ask her questions, make changes. The Human Resources (HR) has to review it, ask questions, make changes. If we're lucky, no one will ask for additional justification or rewrites of job descriptions and we can move forward with advertisements. The ad needs to be written for social media and approved by the HR. Of course, we have to advertise the job in-house, first, in the interest of fairness so that all the night school people can apply. Then we can place the ad and await the cover letters and resumes. After 10 to 20 candidates are selected for a close look, 5 to 10 are selected for the interview.

In Any Event, Remember These Things

You can't make yourself completely into the person someone else wants you to be. With that in mind, it is important to believe in the following:

1. You are at a job interview to interview your prospective employer as much as the employer is there to interview you. If you agree with this statement, you should also agree to these.
2. If you aren't prepared to walk away from the job offer, don't negotiate.
3. If you can't be the kind of person you are at an interview, you don't want to work there.
4. Any company is only as good, or as bad, as its employees.
5. You are a talented person. You deserve respect, dignity, hospitality. If you don't get that kind of treatment, walk away, fast.
6. There is a perfect job for everyone.
7. Money is a negative motivator. People who are unhappy and blame it on their salaries are unhappy people.

Let's repeat this: You should not be sitting at an interview thinking, "Please let them hire me." You should be engaged in judging the company as much as they are judging you. You should be asking yourself, "Can I see myself being happy working here every day? Is this the kind of place that shares my values?"

If You Don't Hear From Someone

It's a very good bet that if you don't hear from someone within a month, you're not going to be interviewed. At that point, if you've done everything this book suggests you should move on. They don't like you; they don't want you (or some other equally negative outcome). If, however, you get the magic call and are interviewed, you have a slightly better chance. I say slightly because there are no guarantees you'll get anywhere near the job.

Here's a Trick You Can Use

Let's say you've been interviewed and haven't heard from the company for a while. If that's the case, you probably didn't get the job. Out of sight, out of mind. The offer has been made and the company is waiting for the lucky one to resign and send a letter of commitment (or sign an employment contract). Your rejection letter is sitting on the secretary's desk waiting to be sent to you. If you're like me and can't stand the suspense, here's a tactic.

If it's been more than a week since you heard from them, call the company, tell the secretary you just saw an announcement for the position on social media for a job in his department. (Or, tell him a friend saw the announcement and said you were perfect for the job.) Ask the secretary if you can send a resume, if the job has been filled. He'll give you all the information you need, even if he just says, "Oh, yeah, we just offered that job to someone." Thank him, hang up, swear at the wall.

Don't Burn Any Bridges

Even if you had the worst experience of your life—they made you sit in the lobby for half an hour because the interviewer was late, he, then, cut the interview short by thirty minutes, they forgot to stamp your parking pass and you had to pay, they were outright rude and condescending. If this happens to you, smile and be on your way. You never know when you'll run into them again. Heck, they might even hire you when another job opens. Just as when you thought you did awful on a test but got an "A," you may have made a great impression on them in the interview. Who knows, they may figure in your employment somehow, even if it's idle talk about you at a cocktail party. And, as I said earlier, don't work anywhere you don't want to. Never take a job for the sake of having a job and making money.

Good salespeople build relationships because they never know when they might make a sale. Marketing is more than sales, much more, but in the end, it's all about relationships built on understanding.

Go use marketing to get your dream job! If you need any help, be sure to reach out to me. Write to me at: edbarr@cmu.edu or edwardharrison-barr@gmail.com Good luck!

Abbreviations

Chapter 3
AIDA: Attention, Interest, Desire, Action

Chapter 4
SWOT Analysis: Strengths, Weaknesses, Opportunities, Threats

Chapter 8
B2B: business-to-business

AMA: American Marketing Association

Chapter 11 and 14
HR: Human Resources

About the Author

Edward Barr has taught thousands of people over a 25-year career at Carnegie Mellon University (CMU) in Pittsburgh, PA, USA, where he currently teaches and coaches computational finance majors to communicate better when they take jobs on Wall Street.

Before beginning his career at CMU, he served as a marketing executive in both for-profit and not-for-profit companies for over 20 years, including chief marketing officer at iCarnegie, a CMU for-profit. As a marketing professional, he conducted business in Brazil, Colombia, China, India and the United States.

He has taught in China, India, Amsterdam, London, Kazakhstan, Mexico, and Panama. He has taught corporate executives and staff at Cognizant, an IT service company with over 200,000 employees and Cinepolis of Mexico. He has also taught professional writing, business communication, marketing, negotiation, and strategy.

Index

OTHER TITLES IN THE BUSINESS CAREER DEVELOPMENT COLLECTION

Vilma Barr, Consultant, Editor

- *Fast Forward Your Career* by Simonetta Lureti and Lucio Furlani
- *Rules Don't Work for Me* by Gail Summers
- *Ask the Right Questions; Get the Right Job* by Edward Barr
- *100 Skills of the Successful Sales Professional* by Alex Dripchak
- *Negotiate Your Way to Success* by Kasia Jagodzinska
- *Personal and Career Development* by Claudio A. Rivera and Elza Priede
- *Getting It Right When It Matters Most* by Tony Gambill and Scott Carbonara
- *How to Make Good Business Decisions* by J.C. Baker
- *The Power of Belonging* by Sunita Sehmi
- *Your GPS to Employment Success* by Beverly A. Williams
- *Emotional Intelligence at Work* by Richard M. Contino and Penelope J. Holt
- *The Champion Edge* by Alan R. Zimmerman

Concise and Applied Business Books

The Collection listed above is one of 30 business subject collections that Business Expert Press has grown to make BEP a premiere publisher of print and digital books. Our concise and applied books are for...

- Professionals and Practitioners
- Faculty who adopt our books for courses
- Librarians who know that BEP's Digital Libraries are a unique way to offer students ebooks to download, not restricted with any digital rights management
- Executive Training Course Leaders
- Business Seminar Organizers

Business Expert Press books are for anyone who needs to dig deeper on business ideas, goals, and solutions to everyday problems. Whether one print book, one ebook, or buying a digital library of 110 ebooks, we remain the affordable and smart way to be business smart. For more information, please visit www.businessexpertpress.com, or contact sales@businessexpertpress.com.

www.ingramcontent.com/pod-product-compliance
Lightning Source LLC
Chambersburg PA
CBHW061332220326
41599CB00026B/5149